SAN DIEGO UNTAPPED!

Brewery Tap & Tasting Room
Excursions in America's "Capital of
Craft"

including...
San Diego Historical Spots and
Neighborhood Tour Guide

by Robert A. Bellezza

*Featuring original brewery photos
and book design by the author.*

ISBN: 978-1-7347584-3-6

April 2020

Tour & Travel Media
PO Box 502
Vista, CA 92085
www.californiatourandtravel.com

DEDICATION

Remembering my friend Michael Killagrew's shared
impressions, artistic endeavors, family moments, waterphone blues,
Final Fridays libations and time well-traveled together.

Cheers! My Good Friend

Other California Books by the Author:

Foreword

As I write this in 2017, there are now more than one hundred and fifty brewhouses peppered over the County of San Diego. To put that number in some context, this is an increase of over one hundred and twenty brewhouses in less than a decade.

This "New Brew Wave", a renaissance of local brewing, started at the short lived original incarnation of the Bolt Brewery in Fallbrook in 1987. It was there that they let the local craft beer genie out of the keg and in doing so ended a fallow period of some thirty four years, during in which time no beer was brewed commercially in the county. This brewing renaissance was built primarily on the backs of local home brewers, some of whom took out second mortgages on their homes in order to follow their passion of brewing great beers as they turned "pro". This early group of "micro brewers", as they were then known, generally followed a mantra of "the beer comes first," a true example of quality over quantity which has fortunately been well sustained by those San Diego brewers who have followed in their footsteps.

Over the years that I have researched this history, I have found numerous incidents of amazing happenstance and what some may refer to as providence, the type of which is usually found in the plot lines of legends and fairy tales. In the early days of this renaissance, a zig here or a zag there and this amazing industry would have been stopped dead in its tracks. It also tottered and briefly stalled during the late nineteen nineties during the precipitous downturn of what had been the "micro brewing" boom.
A number of the earlier established local "micro breweries" sadly did fail during this period however, fortunately the foundation had been already been laid and a group of talented brewers emerged from some of these ashes to go on down the trail blazed by the pioneers and help create additional breweries, perhaps even more acutely aware of what was almost lost.

A drive for excellence has over the last couple of decades helped elevate San Diego's brewing to a level where they now win multiple medals in numerous competitions against both domestic and international competitors on a frequent basis. It has also led to a community that is both proud of its communal achievements and exhibits a camaraderie where brewers make extra efforts to help out fellow brewers with ingredients, equipment and a willingness to share knowledge across the board. Too this end, there is also a self policing of any bad beer that might occasionally show up and which may potentially threaten to damage the whole. Other brewers will step in quickly to help rectify any such threat, though with that said, with the current competition in the market place for both tap handles and/or shelf space for those breweries that package, if you brew bad beer in San Diego, unless you have a rich uncle, you will not survive. We have seen San Diego beers and brewers influence brewers both domestically and internationally. The meteoric rise of the IPA craft category across the US has been heavily influenced by the IPAs and the heavily hopped Pale Ales that have and continue to emanate from many San Diego breweries. Although the county is arguably IPA centric, it would be a mistake to think that these are "one trick pony" brewers and to that end there is a wide and diverse array of all styles of excellently brewed beers that will dispel any such notion at the first sip.

I met Bob in San Diego, naturally over a beer when he was doing the research for this book and was instantly taken with his keen and genuine interest in the local brewing community. What's great about Bob's book is that in addition to it being a great snap shot of a moment in time in San Diego brewing history, he has also drilled down into the weeds (hops?) and captured not only information about the beers but some of the nuances of the brewers and their breweries too. If you are reading this book in San Diego County then hopefully you currently have a delicious local brew in your other hand. If you are reading it somewhere else and haven't visited before, then bring it along with you and follow the great beer trail that Bob has researched for you. Come on down, the weather's fine - pretty much always - and I can assure you, the brews are some of the best you'll find anywhere on this planet of ours.

Cheers!

Sheldon M. Kaplan
San Diego

Beer barrels at Eppig Brewery, North Park, San Diego.

North County's local beer enthusiasts congregate at the Booze Bros. main brewery tap and tasting room, in Vista.

Contents

Chapter 1 • Brewery Tap & Tasting Rooms

Chapter 2 • San Diego's Colorful Craft

Chapter 3 • San Diego Brewing Affiliates

Chapter 4 • Historical Spots & Neighborhoods

Addendum

Prohibition's ban on alcoholic beverages lasted over 13 years, through 1933, closing all San Diego brewing industries. After prohibition few breweries came back. By today's count, over 150 craft breweries opened their doors in the last 15 years.

(Courtesy of San Diego Brewing)

A 1920 photograph of the brewery's namesake is on display at the Indian Joe Brewing tasting room. Uncle Joe's ancestral San Diego roots dates to the days of Spain's Alta California mission settlements. (Courtesy of Indian Joe Brewing)

ACKNOWLEDGMENTS

San Diego UnTapped! would not exist without direct input of the brewery owners and brewers themselves. Perhaps, there's not a more sincere group of entrepreneurs more open to discussing the complexities and inner workings to running a small brewery. The content of the book is taken from 75 interviews, directly quoting many details of brewing an artisan's pallet of craft products often extending into interesting commentaries. It supports the many reasons of increasing and nearly infinite possibilities. Better beer dominates the San Diego scene and grown to a peak point of productivity, garnering congregations of increasing devotees at the brewery tap and tasting rooms. Also, on the rise are 'Beercations' with up-close encounters exploring award-winning tasty craft inherent to cultural neighborhoods of San Diego.

Almost 4,000 employees work at the local brewing industries supporting a vigorous upstream economy of culinary, lodging and hospitality businesses. There have been traditions set, including the San Diego International Beer Festival in Del Mar, that showcases the community and the largest beer festival on the West Coast. The craft industry exemplifies the very definition of community and reflective of centuries' old brewing cultures translated into today's world of interconnectivity and modernity. There's few other places as conducive exploring world class attractions and hospitality, a balmy outdoor climate with farm to table satisfaction knowing you're always close in proximity to incredible craft beers and incomparable times to share with friends and family.

INTRODUCTION

San Diego's Colorful Craft

There's an explosion of craft breweries saturating San Diego's landscape due to an extraordinary effort of a valiant group in the professional craft brewing industry. It's an exciting development for local beer enthusiasts and tourists coming to California's southern bay city. If you've not been to San Diego in recent years, there's many reasons for visiting its vibrant seaside climate at the epicenter of professional craft brewing. Each beer is made from four basic ingredients and brewed into a range of classes, styles and flavors. The largest brewing competition on the West Coast, San Diego International Festival, brings attention to San Diego's modern moniker, 'America's Capital of Craft'. Today, 150 local breweries are established with tap and tasting rooms offering many styles of handmade craft beers, produced right at the source. Abundant rewards lie ahead for the average beer lover, and its truly an Eureka! moment for any beer aficionado in search of fresh traditional and concept beers, directly from the brewery's own tasting room taps.

As far back as 1995, only four pioneering craft breweries had existed in San Diego, yet dozens more individual home brewers were joining the generational quest of brewing better beer. Today, we may contemplate dozens of high-quality San Diego breweries, each unique as the people running them. Remarkably, there's an unified air and common thread within the brewing community leaving the impression, "everybody knows everybody." Many are among San Diego's small batch or larger independent craft brewers, equally and competitively linked as one.

The team at award-winning Rip Current Brewing, San Marcos, preparing a fresh kettle of craft beer.

Navigating a rising tide of quality craft beer of San Diego requires circuitous excursions with time for investigating and taste testing, as well as attending many festivals. Often, the brewhouse tasting rooms in San Diego conveniently cluster together in niche neighborhoods and appear in large numbers in North Park, Ocean Beach, North County and notably, Miramar, or belovedly characterized as "Beeramar". San Diego's craft breweries have established numerous satellite tasting rooms offering the thrill of the chase of any county offering the highest numbers of brewery labels and tasting rooms nationally! The inevitability imbibing adventurous one-off flavors, kettle or barrel-aged beer sour styles, magical wild yeasts and fresh beers infused with quality fruit purees or herbs, saisons, sours, hazy or spicy, all are fresh from the tap. Other San Diego specialties includes craft vodka, whiskey, moonshine, bourbon, brandy, mead, sake, soda, and kombucha, each freshly brewed, bottled, and six-packs.

The San Diego climate averages 263 sunny days a year. It's reputation as a destination of beautiful beaches, theaters, museums, farm to table dining serving the freshest craft beers and beverages, many not found on the average supermarket shelves. A far cry from the days of bland homogeneous American 'Big Beer' brands, An amazing odyssey of discovery, each brewery maintains solidarity towards improving the community, striving with a strong commitment brewing quality products. Touring and tasting responsibly, there's an invitation from 'America's Finest City's Capital of Craft Beer' …its most creative craftsman's dedication to World Class hospitality.

MAP OF BREWERY TAP & TASTING ROOM NEIGHBORHOODS

Find the neighborhood breweries you are interested in visiting, then check the main breweries listed in San Diego UnTapped! on the following pages.

Coronado Brewing Company's Knoxville facility has many outstanding choices of craft beers.

SAN DIEGO BREWERY TOURS

OF MAIN BREWERY TAP & TASTING ROOMS - ON NEXT PAGE

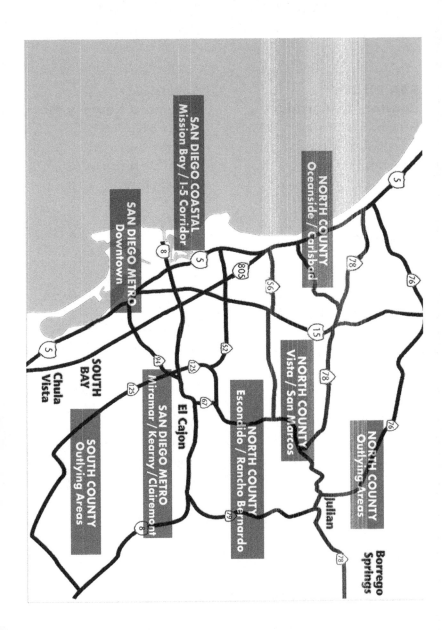

BREWERY TAP & TASTING ROOMS
Breweries Listed by Region

SAN DIEGO
Coastal / I-5 Corridor

Acoustic Ales Brewing Experiment
Amplified Ale Works
Coronado Brewing Company
Ocean Beach Brewery
New English Brewing Co.

SAN DIEGO
Downtown

Bolt Brewery
Citizens Brewers
Groundswell Brewing Co.
Pariah Brewing Co.
San Diego Brewing Co.

SAN DIEGO
Miramar / Kearney Mesa

32 North Brewing Co.
AleSmith Brewing Co.
Duck Foot Brewing Co.
Kilowatt Brewing
Little Miss Brewing
Longship Brewery
Pure Project
Quantum Brewing Co.
Societe Brewing Co.
White Labs Int'l Headquarters

SAN DIEGO
Outlying Areas

Bay Bridge Brewing
BNS Brewing & Distilling Co.
Julian Beer Co.
Nickel Beer Co.
Novo Brazil Brewing Co.
Pacific Islander Beer Co.
Smoking Cannon Brewery

**JOIN FRIENDS & FAMILY FOR TOURING TWO OR MORE
NEIGHBORHOOD CRAFT BREWERIES**

ENJOY BEER MORE!

NORTH COUNTY
Carlsbad / Oceanside

Arcana Brewing Co.
Belching Beaver Brewery
Culver Beer Co.
Golden Coast Mead
Legacy Brewing Co.
Mason Ale Works
Oceanside Brewing Co.
Rouleur Brewing Co.

NORTH COUNTY
Inland / I-15 Corridor

Second Chance Beer Co.
Stone Brewing Co.

NORTH COUNTY
Vista / San Marcos

Abnormal Beer Company
Aztec Brewing Co.
Back Street Brewery
Barrel Harbor Brew Co.
Beach Grease Brewing Co.
Booze Brothers Brewing Co.
Dos Desperados Brewing
Ebullition Brewing Co.
Indian Joe Brewing
Iron Fist Brewing Co.
Latitude 33° Brewing
Prohibition Brewing Co.
Rip Current Brewing Co.
Wild Barrel Brewing Co.

Chapter 1

Brewery Tap & Tasting Rooms in America's "Capital of Craft"

32 North Brewing Co.

8655 Production Avenue, Ste. A
San Diego, CA 92121
619-363-2622
www.32northbrew.com

Steven Peterson, Owner
Samuel Golden, GM/Manager
Jeff Swem, Brewer/Barrel Master
Collier Turley, Brewer

In October of 2014, a new brewery emerged in Miramar introducing the buzz words, "Pour, Drink, Explore!" True to its craft, 32 North Brewing Company invites exploration into the unchartered territory tasting traditional beer styles, highlighting hard to find more adventurous beer flavors. "Our name welcomes people to San Diego's southern latitude and experience 32 North's mission of brewing the highest quality, as well as out of the ordinary beer. "For us, we love making varieties not found anywhere else," accentuates Sam Golden, the taproom manager. "There are a number of prerequisite IPAs brewed at 32 North Brewing, and recently we are concentrating on pilsners and lagers on filling a void. The trend towards taste includes complex flavors in light beer, and big beers like IPAs."

On the left, Steven Peterson heads the 32 North brewing team creating great beer brewed to "Pour, Drink & Explore!" There are new releases every week fulfilling the demand for the love for craft beer.

It takes skill to brew a lighter beer with lower alcoholic volume, and around 5% abv allows a more delicate taste range to dominate the beer. At the brewery tasting room, there are 15 taps with six core beers complimenting the brewery's specialty one-off beer. There are kegs, growlers, and cans to choose, and of course always something new on tap. Collier Turley, Head Brewer, and Jeff Swem, Barrel Master, are allowed freedom to brew up completely different recipes each month. Jeff is working on a barrel aging schedule taking approximately six months to one year before reaching maturity, "so, the beer tells you when it's done." The beer distribution is handled throughout San Diego county and Arizona into tap rooms and restaurants. Sam enthusiastically mentions, "the social aspect at the tap room may be enjoyed by locals and families coming for conversation. There's games to play or relax, and the brewery's dressed down appearance within a 10,000 sq. ft. warehouse becomes a perfect place to offer the latest amusing games. Giant Connect Four oversized Cornhole game, Dart boards, and Giant Jenga, are meant to test your skills. The brewery's support of community services is ongoing." In 2018, the brewery earned a Bronze Medal at the San Diego International Beer Festival for an American-Style Lager, Pilsner the Conqueror.

Ready to be filled at the brewery, 32 North Brewing prefers recyclable cans for specialty beer shipped fresh throughout southern California and Arizona.

The brewery brings food trucks to the door for satisfying gourmet cooking, and 32 North's brewery tap room is open most nights to 10pm. "We can fit up to 215 people in the brewery, so we have movie nights, trivia nights on Thursdays, as well as birthdays, weddings, receptions, even salsa nights. We love fundraisers working with Pints for Paws, Big Brothers Big Sisters, and charities," Sam emphasizes. There's always a one-off experimental beer to find new unique taste and style appeal from specialty hops and yeasts chosen by the 32 North team. Stopping at 32 North Brewing will reveal something new and something about San Diego beer, each and every time.

(Courtesy of 32 North Brewing)

ABNORMAL BEER COMPANY

16990 Via Tazon, Suite 124
San Diego, CA 92127
858-618-2463
www.abnormalcompany.com

ABNORMAL BEER CO

Abnormal Beer Company meets the highest possible expectations of great food and beverage served in San Diego. "The concept of food, a full service wine bar, and brewpub is all about producing beer, wine, and food, through our various companies; Abnormal Beer Co., Abnormal Wine Co., and The Craft & Cork restaurant." The Abnormal Beer Co. was opened in 2015 and in 2018, the brewery earned a Bronze Medal at the San Diego Int'l Beer Festival for an European Lager, named Export. "Our concept pays attention to our brewery's flavor focus and water chemistry, and we bring main ingredients into recipes offering perfect pairings with seasonal food flavors."

Located in the Corporate Center off Rancho Bernardo Road, Cork & Craft's sophisticated atmosphere and comfortable table settings are framed by a long bar facing a tall wall of glass in view of a glistening tank farm. Showcased are over 40 draft taps, serving the finest beer from the area and rotating 8-12 core house beers, along with the freshest Abnormal ales, lagers, and sours. Flavor ingredients are carefully thought out with matching fresh appetizers and entrées. Cork & Craft adheres to San Diego's new paradigm, contributing "abnormally great" food and beverage anticipated in America's Finest City. At the 2017 San Diego International Beer Festival, Abnormal's Tummy Cuddles, a chocolate and chili beer earned a Bronze Medal. The goal has been consistent, "as we are attracting people getting into beer, and younger crowds are coming to bottle releases, and we're rated one of two top-rated brewpubs by Untappd and Beer Advocate."

Visitors might attend an Abnormal Dinner Series debuting fresh craft beer with quality gourmet pairings. Abnormal Brewery Co. opened their doors April 7, 2015, and soon voted best brewpub in West Coaster magazine the next year. There are 3 main Abnormal labels, IPA, Stout, 5PM session beer; plus, the brewery produces 1000 bottles a month of specialty beer, barrel-aged beer and sours. "After we strip back the water using reverse osmosis, we add back certain minerals for each beer. Each beer has a unique water profile," and at the brewery, "we keep oak whiskey casks as part of our barrel program consistently making one-off specialty beer we bottle. We'll offer a wide range of beer, and we don't hold back with the variety of sours we produce. Approachability to fine beer is most important."

ACOUSTIC ALES BREWING EXPERIMENT

1795 Hancock Street, Suite P1
Tasting Room
2120 W. Washington St.
San Diego, CA 92110
619-299-2537
www.acousticales.com

Tommaso Maggiore, Owner

Acoustic Ales Brewing Experiment tap and tasting room occupies an upper level at the historical brick Mission Brewery Building, near San Diego's airport, just off I-5.

In 2013, Acoustic Ales Brewing Experiment met the challenge reoccupying the renovated 100-year old Mission Brewery building, reestablishing the building's original plan as a brewery. The famous five-story brick facility, completed in 1912, had been established during a short lived era with a sudden halt brought by the era of Prohibition. Acoustic Ales Brewing Experiment is known for its excellent ales, one-of-a-kind beer, and acclaim from fans all over the West Coast including the L.A., Orange County, Northern California, Arizona, and Oregon. Tommaso Maggiore, owner of Encinitas Ale House and The Public House in La Jolla, founded Acoustic brewery and uses the added benefits of local farming

In San Diego at Hancock & Washington Streets, the Acoustic Ales Brewing Experiment tasting room is street level from the stairs of Mission Brewery Plaza.

for brewing with the freshest fruit-hopped flavors and local honey. Serving from its 13 taps, 2 nitro, and 3 casks at the tap and tasting room's street level pub located at the corner of Hancock & Washington Streets, the tasting room features innovative craft beer offering with varied styles of tasty brews to choose from keeping your palate hoppy and happy. Acoustic Ales consistently brings new interesting beer to the table. In 2013-2014, the brewery won two Gold Medals two years in a row at Del Mar's San Diego International Beer Festival for their Honey Nut Brown Ale, an American Strong. They also earned 2015's Silver Medal for a tasty rye beer, Back N The GSSR, made exclusively with hops imported from New Zealand and Australia.

By 1915, the Mission brewery building transitioned to making a non-alcoholic malt and hop soft drink called "Hopski" over a brief period. By late 1919, Prohibition's 18th Amendment had doomed all San Diego breweries. After the 1986 earthquake, the recent craze in San Diego craft beer gave a more immediate purpose bringing the building back to former splendor after a complete structural renewal. There's a convenient bus stop at the intersection of Hancock and Washington, with signs to the tasting room's door visible on the corner. The landmark brick building is easy to spot off the I-5 corridor, near the airport, with its vintage mission revival industrial architecture as a one-of-a-kind classic in San Diego's turn of the century history.

A San Diego landmark, the Mission Brewery Plaza was built in 1912, and has housed breweries, a hospital, a kelp processing agar plant and commerical offices.

Belching Beaver Brewery celebrates its opening at its newest facility and tasting room in Oceanside's Corporate Center. There are five current San Diego County locations including a landmark brewpub in a remodeled bank building in downtown Vista.

Legendary brewer, Peter Zien with his wife Vicky, have nurtured AleSmith Brewing Company into one of the most recognized craft breweries of San Diego. The brewery features award-winning craft beers, barrel-aged beers, sours and handmade cheeses.

Recently, North County's Booze Bros. downtown Oceanside satellite tasting room, has opened on Mission Ave.

ALESMITH BREWING COMPANY

9990 Alesmith Court
San Diego, CA 92126
858-549-9888
www.AleSmith.com

Peter & Vicky Zien, Owners

July 2002, as a act of mercy, Peter Zien was prepared to bring back to life a small craft brewery in Miramar, AleSmith Brewing Company and rescue a jewel in the rough from the brink of oblivion. Today, AleSmith Brewing stands at the center of the craft beer renaissance,

and a legendary San Diego saga continues moving into the future. Peter recalled from the brewery's inception in 1995, "at the time only three other craft breweries had been operating. AleSmith's ship would take over 13 years to stay the course from the opening day. I always loved good beer, but it wasn't until I picked up that brew paddle and made my first batch, I realized beer is the blend of art and design I'd been looking for my whole life. I didn't want to be a lawyer, I wanted to make beer and enjoy the creativity with people I knew, and it's been a hell of a good ride."

AleSmith's full ascension as a model San Diego brewery was the direct result of expert brewing recipes, skill, and great management. A major league brewer, Peter Zien achieved the first highest ranking of a Grand Master Level 1 Certified Beer Judge in San Diego. He remains the visionary of AleSmith and a guiding force behind San Diego's craft brewing industry's recent rise to fame. The small brewery originally was located in a warehouse off Miramar Rd. on Cabot Dr., established by brewmasters Skip Virgilio and Ted Newcomb. From its humble beginnings, AleSmith began adding small measures of success from brewing competitions in 1998. Winning a Bronze Medal at the

Great American Beer Festival, or GABF, for a Belgian Golden Strong Ale had become a significant victory for San Diego's early branding of West Coast craft styles. Peter's years of paying homage to centuries old traditions brewing craft beer would work well in adding character and creativity to the brewery's best products.

AleSmith Brewing jumped into hyper-gear with recognition in 2008 at the Great American Beer Festival earning "Small Brewing Company Award", and the highest honor as the GABF "Brewer of the Year". By 2016, over AleSmith's lifetime 18 medals have been earned at the GABF including 3 Gold Medals awarded to AleSmith's Old Numbskull Barley Wine-style Ale successively in 2013, 2014 and 2016. And in 2008, AleSmith earned dual Gold Medals for a Strong Scotch Ale, AleSmith Wee Heavy and a Strong Ale, Decadence Old Ale. Triumphantly, at the most recent 2018 San Diego International Beer Festival, AleSmith Brewing earned two silver medals, adding to top honors as 2017's "Champion Brewer" as well as carrying home Gold Medals for Private Stock British-style Strong Ale, and Old Numbskull Barley Wine.

As a result of the accelerating pace of the craft beer market in 2014, AleSmith began planning upgrades and moving brewery operations to a new home base, again off Miramar Rd. at 9990 AleSmith Court. Operations began at the new brewery in March 2015, and the new tasting room opened in October. The brewery's total footprint measures a massive 105,000 sq. ft., and Peter's sophisticated touch designing the brewery matches well with his wife Vicky's talents. They work together as a team running one of the largest tasting rooms in San Diego, and day to day operations at AleSmith. The role Vicky and Peter play positively contributes to AleSmith's future everyday. Recently, they've opened a community meeting center in the upper tier above the tasting room's western wall. It offers a large gathering and banquet space seating up to 125 people. Both Peter and Vicky intend to make a difference surrounded by an active team of diversified employees. A chance arrangement brought recent Sudanese immigrants to AleSmith's employment. As the head of Human Resource Department, Vicky attended a church gathering and had been introduced to the "Lost Boys of Sudan." She hired ten of the boys after she discovered, "the church was seeking employment opportunities for thousands forced out south Sudan during the civil war going for 15 years. As refugees, they survived walking a 1000 miles, and most had lost their parents or don't even know their birthdays."

Brewing equipment and giant kettles manufactured by a 150-old Germany company are used exclusively at AleSmith.

AleSmith's premiere beer introduced after long hibernation aging in wooden bourbon barrels was christened Speedway Stout and became the first core line at the brewery. It has become a hallmark modern day classic remaining highly lauded as a barrel-aged beer with a smooth rich and ominous pitch-black appearance at 12% abv. In 2008, Speedway Stout brought home a Silver Medal from the Great American Beer Festival for Aged Beer. It achieved pure Gold in 2012's San Diego International Beer Competition and again Gold in 2014, as the best Imperial Stout.

In tribute to a San Diego legend and Padres' great Tony Gywnn, AleSmith has enshrined a permanent memorial and world class baseball museum inside the AleSmith tasting room. It's a special recognition to Tony's career. The museum houses many memories from the legacy of Tony's past with the San Diego Padres as a player and manager. The museum is built within the tasting room in it's own temperature controlled environment. The interior provides artful circular showcases displaying the iconic player's amazing memorabilia collected during his lifetime. The collection includes game jerseys, signed team baseballs, championship rings, and many personal possessions honoring a great San Diego Padre and special friend of the brewery. It links the San Diego's brewing industry's love of baseball by dedicating a new beer at AleSmith directly

At the heart of the AleSmith brewing, a Krone German system facilitates quadrupling brewing capacities for the future.

honoring Tony Gwynn. Peter and Vicky worked directly with Tony and the Gywnn family over years and decided on a recipe for a special ale. AleSmith's San Diego .394 Pale Ale commemorates Tony's lifetime batting average with his personal touch to the popular new IPA under the AleSmith label. It's sale supports the memory of the San Diego legend and The Tony and Alicia Gwynn Foundation. Founded in 1995, it's services have helped thousands of people overcome obstacles with family, work and housing.

Peter's long time affinity with the Southern California music scene has worked plans up for another new beer release available at the brewery. An agreement with the band Sublime, AleSmith is brewing a commemorative label and homage to the 25-year anniversary release of the Long Beach band's 40 Ounces to Freedom, a well known anthem of surf, rock, suds and music fans throughout the South Coast. AleSmith's 40 oz. limited release special Mexican style lager beer memorializes the group's enduring popularity. The new beer is available in six packs.

Peter Zien remains an esteemed member of
QUAFF, the Quality Ale & Fermentation
Fraternity, San Diego's most prominent
home brewing club. Showcasing his
accomplishments as a home brewer
professionally, he works today in the capacity
of a certified BCJP Judge. The skills he
gathered home brewing reflect on the
handmade artistry of brewing beer over the
years as a professional. Honoring tradition
brewing from scratch ingredients and strictly

adhering to only best quality, AleSmith's popularity continues to grow as a small
craft brewery. The recent expansion planning increased production projects
reaching over 200,000 barrels a year relies on a newly installed imported Krone
German brewing system. The new brewing kettles and fermentation tanks
feature a completely closed-system technology ensuring consistent pure quality
while fine tuning each step during the brewing process. Adding an automated
in-house bottling plant will fill 35 bottles at a time and output up to 400 bottles
a minute, also sanitizing, filling and capping the freshest beer ready for the
worldwide marketplace. Peter elaborates initial brewing processes, "and the base
malt silo holds 90% of brewing grain. The magic 10% of specialty malts impart

colors and flavors, and they're
still brought in by the bag. Our
grains come from the best malting
companies all over the world
including Germany and England.
They are milled here at the
brewery, and rollers gently crack
the grains to not pulverize them,
so the husks remain in the mash
covering the kettle's false bottom,
or you may end up with a stuck system. Every step, even the milling is carefully
performed, and the grain goes straight up in vertical buckets dropping down in
the closed system, ready for brew day and fed into the mashtun."

Peter Zien's innovations are uniquely matched to America's fascination for all
things 'Breweriana!' The tasting room mirrors a stadium design with a dugout,
bleachers, and a special baseball museum. At the small niche bar Anvil & Stave

are samplings of aged sours and specialty reserve beer made at AleSmith. Peter's connection with nearby dairy farmers has built good relationships through the brewery's donation of its spent grain for dairy feed and completes a natural cycle reusing brewery byproducts. Keeping the ball rolling, Peter spent the last 15 years developing special artisanal skills becoming a craft cheesemaker. Visualizing a love for pairing craft cheeses with specialty beer, he's expanded space in the brewery for a gourmet cheese manufacturing facility. Peter's CheeseSmith introduces a line of handmade cheese, and a community stopping off place for discovering new products at AleSmith. As Peter sums up, "over the last decades, I've been a cheesemaker, and it's become an emerging passion and goal. I'll be debuting great handmade cheeses here at the brewery very soon."

Year-round, seasonal, and barrel-aged brews are represented by several styles. Many are session beers or stronger, and 11 core beers feature a wide range of styles. There are presently six seasonal ales and four barrel-aged available at the brewery. Not unlike his historical predecessor and model citizen brewer, Fritz Maytag's dramatic rescue of San Francisco's craft Anchor Steam Beer, nearly 52 years before him, Peter remains a vital member of the San Diego brewing community and recognized as a brewer with honest respect for the meaning of true craftsmanship.

2019 Competitive Awards Received by AleSmith Brewing

Great American Beer Festival, Denver
Gold Medal - Old Ale or Strong Ale - Private Stock Ale

San Diego International Beer Festival
Gold Medal - American-Style Brown Ale - AleSmith Nut Brown

AMPLIFIED ALE WORKS

Amplified Ales Pacific Beach
Beer Garden and Brew Pub
4150 Mission Blvd. #208
San Diego, CA 92109
858-270-5222

Miramar Tasting Room
9030 Kenamar Drive #309
San Diego, CA 92121
858-800-2534

East Village Tasting Room
1429 Island Ave.
San Diego, CA 92101
619-458-9443

www.amplifiedeales.com

Alex Pierson, Owner

Perched above Pacific Beach's oceanfront, Amplified Ale Works has become a rock star of great West Coast food, craft ale and beer pairings.

A short block from beachfront properties, Amplified Beer Garden & Brewpub patio's elevated view is the place to relax and soak in the sights and suds of Pacific Beach. Co-founders, J.C. Hill and Alex Pierson opened their first restaurant, California Kebab, in 2009 at San Diego State University, then transferred the concept to a tasting room and brewpub, overlooking the ocean at Pacific Beach in 2012. The restaurant serves farm fresh dining from scratch ingredients. Recently, the brewing team won a Silver Medal with their Amber Lager - Vienna Gadda Da Vida at the San Diego International Beer Festival.

Complimenting inspired California Mediterranean-style preparations, Amplified's list of diversified crafted beer includes hop-forward West Coast styles and sessionable lagers. Head brewer Cy Henley, and Director of Brewing Operations, Jeff Campbell, dedicate their focus towards serving a community-centric gathering place for enjoying surf and sun with great food and beer. Special recognition for Amplified's Whammy Bar Wheat earned the brewery a Gold Medal at the 2016 World Beer Cup, honoring their American-style Wheat beer. Another win at the 2017 San Diego International Beer Festival delivered a Bronze Medal for Nyctophobia Barrel-Aged Strong Stout.

With a beer collaboration combining a highly-amped Motorhead album release and concert will be toasted to by two high-volume Amplified ales. The tap room manager explains, "Amplified's strong hoppy pale, Electrocution, and Born to Lose, are boldly aggressive West Coast style ales premiering Motorhead's events in Spring 2017, celebrating their new album, Through the Ages. For now, Motorhead's pilot beer can be found only in San Diego on draft right here."

In 2016, Amplified Ale Works opened their second location, a 7-barrel brewery with a second tap and tasting room in Miramar. In order to bring freshness and quality to the table as one part of a 3-phase plan meeting the brewery's objectives, other projects include tripling the brewery's equipment and a bottling line for packaging new beer. Amplified beers also are using a breakthrough enzyme cultured by the local laboratory, White Labs, called Clarity Ferm. Amplified's former assistant brewer, Garrett Reed, was affected with celiac disease and soon led to blind taste tests, discovering proof positive towards the reliability of reduced gluten-free beer enabling anyone with the problem to enjoy awesome beer without concerns. San Diego's critics and sideways beer reviews alike are always in agreement about Amplified Ale Work's quality and their open invitation. "Whether you're in Miramar just for a beer or enjoying lunch with us down at the beach… we hope to hang with you." Cheers!

ARCANA BREWING COMPANY

5621 Palmer Way, Ste. C
Carlsbad, CA 92010
Phone: (909) 529-2337
www.arcanabrewing.com

Daniel Guy,
Founder / Brewmaster

A remarkable nano-brewery tour in North County San Diego begins at Arcana Brewing Company. A whimsical journey celebrates the discovery of tasty ales, the uniqueness of life, and the workings of a master brewer's handcrafted specialties. Made on a smaller 3-1/2 barrel system, each beer pays tribute to traditional craft beer offered in an array of styles. Daniel Guy's highly complex beers are composed largely with an English bent, served in a setting reminiscent of a vintage pub. There's an enjoyable San Diego Saison, potent porter, and strong ale, as well as frequent small batch beers with unexpected ingredients choices.

The imagery behind Guy's beer titles complements the pure anticipation awaiting each freshly poured glass. By the mug, glass, or flight of four, Arcana's flavors are consistently crafted to never disappoint. The recipes contain malt flavors combining sweetness and bitterness with more seasonal flavors, as a Dark Cherry Winter Ale, Voyager English Ale, and even a Blue Heather Braggot Mead, each a testament to Guy's ingenuity.

A noteworthy IPA, Headbasher India Pale Ale is a favorite selection for an awesome gluten-reduced West Coast style brew. Arcana's Fly Guy Rye IPA compared with other hoppy red San Diego craft brews reveals hints of its rye character mixed with citrusy hops, leaving a sharper, spicier combination of flavors. Capping off a flight with Annabelle's Porter reflects magnificent porter colors delivering smooth flavors to the palette.

North County's Arcana Brewing is in the Carlsbad Gateway Center, four miles from downtown Carlsbad Village.

It has to be somewhat humorous brewing a bacon beer, but Arcana's 'Merica Bacon Ale is popular during September's Bacon Fest in San Diego, especially with it being vegan-friendly with bacony tastiness. San Diego's 2013 and 2015 International Beer Festivals awarded Arcana Brewing Bronze Medals for the Sage Saison for Unique Ingredient Beer, Flying Monkey Braggot for the Other Mead category, and Marley's Ghost for Specialty Beer.

Arcana's customers arrive, often claiming their own handcrafted ceramic mug masterpiece by local potter Jesse Martin. For members of the Mug Club, there are artfully designed beer mugs hung on the brewery's tall background wall. The mug's proud owner collects his or her vessel on entering, reveres, and uses it. Visitors wait in line to become members and own a one-of-kind mug, well aware there's high demand. Members and guests gather in the brewery's muted interior colors, charm, and charisma of the brewery's interior "Steampunk" Middle Earth- style collage. It's been Guy's experience and the Arcana theme emphasizing "Drink Well & Do Good Work", always adding reward and fulfillment to visiting the brewery.

AZTEC BREWING COMPANY

2330 La Mirada Dr. #300
Vista, CA, 92081
800-706-6324
www.aztecbrewery.com

John Webster, Owner / Marketing
Claudia Faulk, Owner / Events
Paul Naylor, Head Brewer

John Webster, Claudia Faulk, and their son, Tristan, had a vision in 2008 bringing Aztec Brewery back in business. The bustling brewery of 1920 was once established by San Diegans circumventing prohibition, beginning a long history just across the border as Azteca Brewery in Mexicali, Mexico. It

Vintage A.B.C. bottle

became Aztec Brewing after moving to San Diego's Barrio Logan at the dawning of post-prohibition in 1933, soon growing to the 3rd largest U.S. brewery west of the Rockies. In 1948, Aztec was sold to Altes Brewing Co. and the brand was retired in 1953. A modern rebirth of Aztec Brewing has brought a renaissance revival to the vintage brewery on La Mirada Road, in Vista. At the forefront of innovation, Head Brewer, Paul Naylor brews traditional beer and seasonally limited editions. Also, Paul has researched ingredients of vintage beer made by early American breweries in order to replicate style possibilities of San Diego's historical Aztec Brewing Company.

Today's Aztec team displays an amazing array of craft flavors honoring the brewery's namesake, especially in traditional styles enhanced with freshly sourced ingredients. In competition at the San Diego International Beer Festival, the brewery garnered Gold Medals in 2012 and 2014, and a Silver Medal in 2013, for Paul's perfected Altbier, Aztec Amber, a traditional German style, popular long before lagers were in style. Seasonal releases to look for include Aztec's magical witch series, Bruja Rosa with

The Blonde Witch marks one of a series of barrel-aged beer celebrating the brewery's 5th Anniversary.

cherries, Bruja Rubia, sour with apricot in 22oz bottles. Another Aztec barrel
-aged sour, Funk #Four - Funky Sour, became the winner of 2016's Gold
Ribbon at the San Diego International Beer Festival. The sours are served in
season and bottled only at the brewery tasting room. Core beers include Aztec's
traditional styles made with unique recipes leaning towards pungent southwest
flavors. A perfect example Aztec Chipolte IPA was sourced by Claudia in
New Mexico for roasted Chipolte peppers. Claudia points to "a smoky, sweet
characteristic from roasted peppers comes out in the brew, although we don't
need to use a lot. Another favorite, Noche de los Muertos Imperial Stout, has a
hint of cinnamon, dark and complex malts, with a balanced hop bitterness and
earthiness. It was a Bronze Medal winner in 2013 at the San Diego International
Beer Festival."

The brewery's mainstay beer includes El Dorado Blonde, very close to a true
kölsch style, and it's crisp, clean taste is an easy brew to drink. Inspired by the
Aztec's mythical city of gold, El Dorado has slight wheat malt characteristics
adding to a balanced bitterness beneath the light grapefruit character of Cascade
hops. And, El Dorado Aztec Coffee Blonde, is a golden blonde ale with added
Mayan coffee blend. Other favorite beers at Aztec Brewing are Sacrifice, a bold
malty Red IPA; and Hop Serpent IIPA, a double bitter Imperial IPA that peaks

Azteca Brewing, pre-prohibition was owned by San Diegans and established after the passing of 1919's Prohibition laws only a short distance across border in Mexico.

at 103 ibu. It's brewed from a blend of American and Australian hops adding hints of fruitiness to its toasty malt. Specialty beer Lemon Ginger Blonde has a twist of lemon and ginger brewed with hibiscus and unfiltered wheat beer, reflecting its roots of a Mexican hibiscus tea. There's a refreshing hefeweizen, with slight hop presence, a light malt complexity and tartness from ginger and added spices. There's also a dessert beer Macaroon Nut Brown Ale, a brown ale brewed with coconut and vanilla. Visitors may sample flights with four tasters, and purchase growler fills,

bottles, cans, and kegs, while enjoying live music at the brewery run by Tristan each week. Come in and bring your friends for Aztec Eatz, and days with appearances from local quality Food Truck specialties including Leo's Mexico City Cuisine, Full Metal Burgers, and Devil Dog BBQ, among others.

BACKSTREET BREWERY

15 Main St. #100
Vista, CA 92083
760-407-7600
www.lamppostpizza.com

April 2004, Back Street Brewing became a stop for lunch and dinner with a beer. Conveniently in Vista's downtown next door to Cinépolis, the brewpub has set a standard of excellence serving craft beer, stouts, IPAs, and tasty pizzas. The manager, Darren Bell explains, "it began with two brothers from Chicago forty years ago franchising Lamppost Pizza stores. They opened their first brewpub in the late 90s, and then three other breweries including ours. Recently, they started a new distribution center and tasting room in Anaheim." The brewery's 10-barrel system is piloted exclusively by Chris Gort, formerly of Stone Brewing and co-founder of Artifex Brewing. A significant list of fresh beer attracts the insatiable aficionado's appetite for sampling session-styled craft beers. You'll find hoppier IPAs, a Raspberry Berliner Weise, and a specialty mosaic hops rye saison Rendezvous. There's an inspired cream ale house draft Fiesta Horchata, also Heritage Hefeweizen, and the Smoked Habanero with infused habanero peppers in amber ale. Specialties are limited including a blonde and kettle sours in the works. The restaurant serves a vary of pizzas, appetizers, pasta, sandwiches, and entrées. It's a perfect downtown destination to stop at their sunny patio and sample delicious food and a beer.

BARREL HARBOR BREW CO.

2575 Pioneer Ave., Suite 104
Vista, CA. 92081
760-734-3949

'At Ease' @ Barrel Harbor
8990 Miramar Road, Suite 150
San Diego, CA 92126.
858-877-0722
www.barrelharborbrewing.com

Tim St. Martin/CEO

Tim St. Martin's home brewing experience in 1993 became a favorite hobby after finding he could make 2 1/2 cases of fresh full-bodied German beer for around $20.50. "I'm a degreed mechanical engineer, and after I met a home brewer at a corporate campout, I had spotted a ritual of

Barrel Harbor's Mirimar 'At Ease' location.

opening his own hefeweizen beer each night. He's the one who guided me into buying equipment, and I got started."

Tim opened Barrel Harbor Brew Company after being stationed in West Germany during the 1980's and familiarizing himself with beer he loves brewing today. Specializing in dunkels, altbiers and hefeweizens, he won a Gold Medal at 2017's San Diego International Beer Festival in Del Mar for the Belgian-style Strong Ale Rungnir, and for his English-style Brown Ale, Barrel Harbor Brown Ale, Bronze medals in 2014 & 2016. Following up in 2018 at the San Diego Int'l Beer Festival, the brewery earned a Silver Medal for its Fruit Style, Funky Buss, and another Silver for an Aussie styled, San Dingo Pale Ale. There's a full array of brewed flavors adhering to the **Reinheitsgebot** (the German beer purity law) following a natural propensity for whole grain combinations.

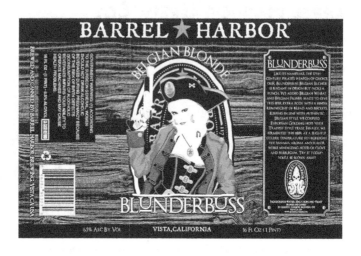

Tim recalls, "between 2009-2010 the neighborhood Fire Chief, ranking one above my brother in San Diego, was a home brewer. Dave and I were discussing how to start up a brewery as he was nearing retirement. We had a concept, names, and loose business plan, finally 2012; he was serious about leaving the Fire Department." One engineer working at the corporate office became interested as an investor as did Tim's brother in law, and they formed the group of four with a solid plan. Tim points out, "as a team, we choose Barrel Harbor, with the lagoons of San Diego so near. A second tasting room was opened in 2016 and formed another partnership between an old friend, and features a tap room on Miramar Rd." The head brewer is Lance McCoy, a brewer with Green Flash for 5 years, and 3 years as shift brewer on Green Flash's new 50-barrel system installed around 2010. Tim emphasizes, "We have entered the GABF and Brewers Association World Beer Cup, and came out with two bronze and a silver for our North English-style Brown Ale. We'll use up to 30 to 35 proprietary recipes, but keep eight core beers on tap year 'round."

Core beer is defined by Barrel Harbor's 8 flagship brews. Fenris IPA, a name of a terrifying wolf in Norse mythology, and Tropical West Coast IPA with complex flavors. South Island Pilsner with 100% German malt is fermented with Czech lager yeast and canned and distributed. Tim's style selections also include Belgian Blunderbuss Blonde, and a brown ale, Little Nugget IPA, and Thunderclap Imperial Stout on tap with other new releases, the tasting rooms are open daily.

BAY BRIDGE BREWING

688 Marsat Court #B
Chula Vista, CA 91911
619-934-7371
www.baybridgebrewing.com

Jim Shirey Co-owner / Brewer
Doug Chase Co-owner / Brewer

If you are traveling as far south as you can go in San Diego County near the Mexican border, it's probably time to stop for a cold one at Chula Vista's friendly neighborhood brewery. One day in 2006, the town would witness a momentous Grand Opening celebrating the very first micro-brewery and craft beer in town. The regional population of Chula Vista makes up the second largest neighborhood next to San Diego metro. According to Jim Shirey, co-founder and brewer, "Bay Bridge Brewing is the farthest south of any other San Diego brewery, and first in Chula Vista. They had to rewrite the city books to accommodate a professional brewery because we were a different type of industry. And today, we're kid and pet friendly, making it a great place for us in the surrounding community."

Jim, and co-owner, Doug Chase started home brewing in 1996, and accumulated a backyard filled from equipment bought from Ballast Point's supply store. Home brewing gathered repeated rave reviews, and eventually they considered opening a professional microbrewery over years. Once, through the grapevine word of La Jolla's Sport City Cafe was closing and selling out brewing business equipment, Jim and Doug decided on acquiring their first professional equipment. After city's approval of the brewery, they found there's a definite edge founding a brewery in a warmer southern location like Chula Vista. It's a place for thirsty folks to relax and enjoy cold Bay Bridge beer, and today's brewing team runs a full-scale system making fresh beer each week. "We're not interested in trendy fads, and we always have 12 beers on tap. None will hit you over the head...and our IPAs are carefully brewed as American, not West Coast. We like to say we do traditional beers and do them very well. We start with Wolf Canyon Wheat on tap, and it won a Gold Medal in 2012. There's the light refreshing Bonita Blonde, and it won a Bronze Medal." Favorite core beers include Star of India IPA, Palomar Pale Ale, America's Finest Amber, and

Bay Bridge Brewing's Chula Vista location has the distinction of being the southern most San Diego craft brewery.

Bill of Rights Red IPA, and winner of a Silver Medal in 2010. Jim's specialty is a Mexican style Horchata Wheat, a beer that's different than any other using natural ingredients without extracts or oils. Jim relates, "typically they use rice milk or flour, but our recipe uses none. It's identical to a taco shop style, and has great mouth feel; but, we came up with all natural ingredients blending malt, cinnamon and vanilla. We self-distribute to bars and restaurants, and some 800 cases were shipped recently to Malaysia in bottles. The beer must be kept cold to keep fresh, so the foreign shipment had refrigeration guaranteed to us. Otherwise, using pasteurization or preservatives changes the flavors."

There are many fundraising events keeping the brewery busy. They participate in April on Earth Day, as well as charity events held for neonatal research, Miracle Baby, on the same weekend. There are several others including local Bonita Fest, an annual Chili Cook-off street fair. The brewery is located off Jaclyn, in the South Rail Business Park of Chula Vista and features food trucks on site each weekend, and every Saturday live bands perform at the brewery. Friday is comedy night and Thursday is trivia night. "There are two breweries opening up on 3rd Avenue in Chula Vista downtown, and they are beer centric bars. We are seeing a craft beer renaissance just awakening here." It's a worthwhile visiting Chula Vista, the most southern location for a chilled beer. Jim and Doug agree at Bay Bridge Brewing, "we're the Cheers of Chula Vista!"

The brewery's head brewer, Paul, and owners, Claudia and John, have been brewing together a decade.

A short seven miles from the Mexican border, Chula Vista's first brewery, Bay Bridge Brewing was opened in 2006. It features weekly music, comedy and trivia nights with great craft beer.

Dave & Donny Firth began Booze Brothers Brewery in 2013, as a gathering place for friends trying out great handcrafted beer and sours.

At Beach Grease Beer Co., you're in your element with any DIY projects when the urge comes, so sit back and enjoy a compatible brew while considering it.

Beach Grease Beer Co.

1280 Activity Dr. at Specialty Dr.
Vista, CA 92081
760-295-7984
www.beachgreasebeerco.com

Owner and CEO, James Banuelos

The Beach Grease Brewery front entry features the mural by "Burrito Breath" making a portal into the brewery tap and tasting room's gallery of skate, surfing, classic cars and rolling art.

Entrepreneur CEO, James Banuelos can elaborate on the reasons for his beer's bump in popularity. "We stay true to West Coast style beers that quench your thirst when it's warm outside. Being a California coastal lifestyle beer brand… they are poundable, sessionable, low abv, refreshing, and always tasty. They're best when working on your hot rod, building your motorcycle, or you're at the beach, you're surfing, you're skateboarding. Well balanced, crisp and refreshing."

Established in 2018, San Diego's Beach Grease Beer Co. is located among Business Park Drive's cluster of craft breweries in Vista, and its successes have created a tidal wave distributing its brand to Orange, LA Counties, and beyond. It's a business model run by numbers that speaks for itself. "Prior to me entering the market with my brand, for years the big craze was very high

Tasting taps at Beach Grease bar, among the brewery's artwork filling in the enormous warehouse.

abv 'pallet wreckers' and heavy heavy beers. For me, not being a brewer, I knew what I wanted and what my friends wanted. And, that's what I had in mind when I started the brand. Because the business is still growing, we will continue to collaborate with major brands featuring our beer as a way of reaching our audience directly."

Beach Grease employs the compelling artwork by Orange County's Juan Murate, for his identifiable generational graphics and high energy flowing forms relating to California's coastal lifestyle of 'climate driven' beer. James' creativity has minted specific beer releases in support of several alliances and collaborations along with well known brands and community non-profits. There are eclectic and esoteric beer names featuring an iconic skateboarder, surfing pro, venerable tattoo artist, even industrial machines and celebrated music groups. "We are originating products at the brewery that coincide with our surroundings. We do what is a reflection of our lives and from subcultures we have been part of. A prime example is La Vuelta, a non-profit Chicano resource that gives 100% of their proceeds back to the community. We did a La Vuelta Hopper Lager at 4.8% abv, packaged and kegged it. Premiering at their annual low rider event in Barrio Logan, it sold really well throughout San Diego. I don't believe in creating campaigns and designs from things I have not been part of, or making money from a life I did not partake in or assist in cultivating."

Stopping by the brewery's impressive industrial size warehouse takes in a world devoted to iconic forms reflective of the founder's background in Santa Cruz around Rat Rods, Hot Rods, custom-built choppers, hand-designed skate and surfboards. The brewery has room to relax, mingle, and enjoy conversations at its tasting bar, long bar and picnic tables. It's also an exotic gallery full of contemporary artforms reiterating James' innovative philosophy. "We're a company and beer brand. We stay true to our DNA and our story, at the same time listening to our consumers. For instance, when we developed recipes for

popular hazy IPAs, we were told they would die off as a fad and at the time they were not even a sanctioned style by GABF. They are on tap over two years so far, and Surf Zombie Hazy IPA with a 6.8% abv features hop forward style of Mosaic and Simcoe, and up and coming hop varietal, Eukanot. It's a hazy with overwhelming notes of papaya, hints of pineapple and a slight resinous background. The beer drinks incredibly smooth, maintaining the expected tropical fruit flavor while avoiding the bitterness of old school IPAs."

Its next of kin, the darker, Crusin' For A Boozin' IPA, at 6.8% abv, is brewed from the freshest Amarillo and Ekuanot hops, conveying a bright aroma and crisp taste to awaken your inner savage soul. The lineup includes, Surf Mummy, at 5.3% abv, a true West Coast hop forward ale brewed from Amarillo, Simco and Cascade hops. A dank and resinous pale ale, it has hints of grapefruit with pine overtones. Filling out IPA choices, Surf Reaper Golden Ale has a strong West Coast hop character featuring hints of citrus, papaya and stone fruit from Citra and Mosaic hops, and balanced out by a biscuity backbone of Maris Otter malt. Beach Grease brewery brings 'what's in demand' to life, as a way of reaching generations who are exploring 'Coastal Conscious' beers.

Honoring Jason Jessee's bike, his '49 Tibetan Pan with an original wishbone frame, welded together by Jessee, after several near-

death defying experiences. A collaborative beer was dubbed Beach Grease Black Tibetan Pilsner, pouring smooth, clean, and crisp at 4.8% abv built with Jason Jessee's skate and chopper design influences. Others favored flavors at the tasting room on the Pilsner side include Poundable at 4.8% abv with CZ Saaz hops, a German Pilsner malt, and cold brew fermentation offering crisp, clean refreshment, spicy lemon and herbal notes. Pistons & Palms, with 5% abv exudes a clean refreshingly hoppy pilsner taste, and aromas of grapefruit peel and lemon. Preferred by 'light' beer drinkers as well as hop heads, it's a perfect beer for a sunny San Diego day to pound more than a few. Oil & Water, a light body Beach Grease Black Lager, brewed at 4.2% abv contains roasty malt dark notes stopping well short of a stout-level dankness. An absolute American Black Lager provides a good option without unnecessary bulk, dark and mysterious, is still refreshing quenchingly dry. Bury Me A G Double IPA, with an 8% abv is fulfilling, amazingly smooth and crushable with noticeable citrus notes and aroma followed by a resinous finish.

Merging Beach Grease artisanal brands reveals an underground culture of California coastal lifestyle and led to multiple marketing partnership platforms under James Banuelos' adept management and creative eye. Each beer fits into California's coastal evolution epicenter of San Diego's craft. The tasting room's one of kind gallery displays several hand painted surfboards and DIY projects and center of operations for take home crowlers or cans. Over past decades, James' involvement included California's art scene and notable New York shows including LA's Known Gallery Oil and Water, as well as his nurturing art-inspired brands, including Us Versus Them and City Fog.

BELCHING BEAVER BREWERY

Oceanside Production Facility / Tasting Room
1334 Rocky Point Dr.,
Oceanside, CA 92056
760-732-1415
www.belchingbeaver.com

Tom Vogel, CEO
Peter Perrecone, Barrel Master
Troy Smith, Brewmaster
Mark Truex, Director of Sales

Vista Production Facility /
Tasting Room
980 Park Center Drive
Vista, CA 9208
760-599-5892

North Park Tasting Room
4223 30th Street
San Diego, CA 92104
618-282-1062

Vista Tavern & Grill
302 E. Broadway
Vista, CA 92084
760-285-8599

Ocean Beach Tasting Room
4836 Newport Ave
San Diego, CA 92107
760-599-5832

It's not surprising Belching Beaver Brewery has become one of San Diego's best known craft breweries. The original 15-barrel Vista production facility was established in 2012, and their next step led to the Grand Opening of Belching Beaver's Vista brewpub, a tavern grill featuring an incredible 75 taps inside downtown's renovated First National Bank of Southern California. Then, the brewery opened two popular satellite tasting rooms in North Park and Ocean Beach. In early 2017, the crowning achievement came with launching a new headquarters brewing facility in Oceanside's Corporate Center. They have an entirely new central brewing system, bottling line, and tasting room, and the new headquarters enables a brewing capacity supporting all five San Diego tasting room locations. It's the result of careful planning by founders, Tom Vogel, Dave Mobley, and Troy Smith nurturing from its inception Belching Beaver Brewery's entry onto San Diego's scene. CEO, Tom Vogel explains, "the partnership formed from a desire to make great beer and have a good time doing it. There were two things: First, having a brand offering quality craft beer, but whimsical and fun enough to inspire good times. From the Winking Milkman to El Castor de Mariachi, you can see each Beaver has its own individual style

and personality. Second, we wanted to make beer for everyone and all palates."

Recently, Belching Beaver's Brewmaster Troy Smith's delicious IPA, Here Comes Mango has won double Gold Medals. He delivered a Gold at the North American Brewers Association Beer Competition and again at the 2017 San Diego International Beer Competition, in Del Mar. In 2018, they followed with three Gold Medals, Mexican Chocolate Peanut Butter Stout, Kolner Krusher German Style Ale, Batch 2 Sour Ale, and a Bronze for Dubbel Dragon Belgian Style Dark Ale. While advancing craft beer's own traditions, Belching Beaver's wide range of distinct IPAs include easy-drinking blonds, triple IPAs, milk stouts, Imperial stouts, beer sours, and barrel-aged beer pleasing the most refined tastes. At first, the brewery's procuring quality ingredients began with, "not worrying how much it would cost securing top shelf hops, even well before the first location or equipment was installed." Troy Smith's brewing background added to the business acumen of Dave and Tom, merged into a robust team geared towards producing a highly revered end-user experience. Tom likes to say the team effort upholds our maximum standards, "when having a name like Belching Beaver, we better have great beer, or we would become the biggest joke in town. I told Troy that I'd throw beer away and delay opening unless it was perfect. In truth, we had no worries because Troy makes great beer!"

Downtown's Vista brewpub opened in 2016 featuring many other brewer's highly acclaimed craft beer labels. The team agrees, "we appreciate supporting other breweries because we wouldn't be where we're at now without our friends

7.3% Alc/Vol   1Pt. 6Fl.Oz.

in the brewing business." Within an incredible 6,600 sq. ft. building, the old vault was repurposed as a wine cellar, and the safety deposit box room is set up for tavern dining. Catching up to extreme demand for their latest beer changed the initial business model. For two years, the company concentrated on hyper-local distribution and production had been limited. Outside distribution to Hawaii would begin, then moving more beer into chain stores like Costco, Vons and Albertsons entered the picture. Vying for shelf space and widening availability created the next winning business model and jubilant praise of their customers.

Troy Smith's brewing background links personal knowledge of brewing craft beer through the family's ownership of the legendary Coronado Brewing Company, one of five San Diego craft breweries operating in 1996. After attending Chico State University, Troy found part-time work at Butte Creek Brewing Co. and Bison Brewing Company cleaning tanks and kegs. Understanding why craft beer was much more enjoyable an experience rather than "slugging down a cold one" became apparent living in Chico, where California's sophisticated Sierra Nevada Pale Ale is headquartered. The summer of 2010 became a pivotal period working during Coronado's ramping up. His stepdad Rick, landed him a job at Five Points Brewing Company with Clint Stromberg's trade brewing facility inside the historic downtown Mission Plaza near San Diego's airport. "As luck would have it," Troy recalls, "Clint's manager left for over a month in Europe, and I took over all the nuts and bolts operations like harvesting yeast, transferring wort to fermenters, brewing, carbonating, scrubbing down equipment, and polishing tanks." Five Points was a contract brewer of Coronado's, also for Simon Lacey's New English Brewing. Troy's new job filled orders of several styles under an increasing local demand. A year later, Coronado stepped in purchasing the facility, and Troy became a direct employee of Coronado for the next two years. Troy reflects on the transition joining as head brewer, and an owner at Belching Beaver. "While I was contracted working with Coronado, Tom Vogel approached me about an opportunity at Belching Beaver during a poker game. I decided the timing was really good joining to become part owner and working even harder as brewmaster at the newest Vista brewery. At that time, I was brewing five days a week for Coronado, and weekends home brewing for Tom Vogel and Dave Mobley, testing out my recipes. Of course, you'd have to go around and check out other breweries to understand what was out there."

Sheer determination and hands-on skill created Troy's most compelling tastings. The pilot batches were brewed into a series of matched 15-gallon recipes inspiring the decision establishing Belching Beaver Brewery.

Troy's sample brews included double IPA and a milk stout for the first core brewery beer. The rest was Belching Beaver brewing history after a founder's meeting arranged at a coastal bar, Dini's of Carlsbad. Troy asked the bar's owner if he could bring in test kegs for Tom and Dave to pass around and sample Troy's latest to see if any made the cut. The warehouse leasing agent was present and ready to sign the paperwork by the end of the meeting. If the testing went well after taking count, and "if everyone agreed to the beer then we're decided. And, that's how the cookie crumbled. Word got out about the new brewery I was joining, and I decided to jump ship with the good graces of the family." Several competitions honoring Troy Smith's brewing expertise have been ongoing, and 2017's Peanut Butter Milk Stout earned a Gold Medal at the Los Angeles Beer Competition, also highly honored "Best in Show," and "Best New Discovery" at the West Coast Craft Can Invitational in San Carlos, CA. Beavers Milk garnered the 2017 Bronze Medal for a Milk Stout at the Los Angeles Beer Competition and was the only milk stout made in California ending up a winner of two Gold Medals in 2014 and 2015. Troy enjoyed it's flavor because, "I like a milk stout's roasted sweetness, and it's a beer that had caught my attention early on. Beavers Milk Stout is light and refreshing to the taste, frothy and silky at 5.3% abv, and 30 ibu. It's a taste that begins with a light coffee roast tapering into a residual sweetness on the finish. We serve it on Nitro or CO_2 on tap. Our first milk stout became a core brew, and eventually it evolved into another, our irresistible Peanut Butter Milk Stout, that's the one that really took off for us."

Downtown Vista's Belching Beaver brewpub restaurant occupies a 6,600 sq. ft. of a former bank building, serving from an incredible array of 75 taps.

Peter Perrecone's path to becoming Barrel Master at Belching Beaver grew from a love of home brewing and expanding into a highly specialized niche. "I've always liked beer to begin with and Sierra Nevada microbrews were coming to San Diego, like AleSmith caught my attention around 2002. I went to school to study the arts and crafting projects, so by age 21, after talking to Tom Garcia, a brewer at Stone, I began home brewing." Along the way, Douglas Constantiner and Travis Smith, co-owners and head brewer from Societe Brewing, helped with Peter's barrel-aging techniques. Lost Abbey's Tomme Arthur gave further in-depth hands-on experience making sours with proprietary yeasts. "I learned about the complexity of beer meeting Peter Zien, who awarded my beer the 2013 Best in Show for a lambic based raspberry sour. It was one I aged 15 months before bottling, and I've built my reputation on sours." During hibernation over one year, beer sours are tested and tweaked in wine barrels. Later, the beer is dry hopped for acidity and added oxygen levels, then spices and fruit fermenting are used over two months bringing out the flavors. Peter works with different yeast banks throughout the country, often blending them affecting the taste, sometimes using up to 12 strains of brettanomyces and lactobacillus bacteria before creating a finished beer. The program uses recycled American oak and French oak wine barrels, with a focus on Belching Beaver sours recognized as a brand from the taste alone. The Vista downtown taproom on Broadway is supported by a 10-barrel system run by Thomas Peters, its head brewer. There

Belching Beaver's pilot site, downtown Vista. Mix and match great craft beers with an array of bar and full entreé menu choices. There is a adjacent large patio with tables.

are several limited release medal winners of experimental beer including his biggest baddest beer, Pound Town, winning the "Alpha King" award at GABF. Labeled a triple IPA, it chimes in at 10.3% and a full 100 ibu! Among the core beers at Belching Beaver's tap rooms, Hop Hwy IPA commemorates the City of Vista's 50th Anniversary with an India Pale Ale, also a Silver Medal winner at the World Beer Championships in 2014. A new beer and collaboration with the Deftones's Chino Moreno, and Phantom Bride IPA brewed by Thomas is a perfect choice for kickin' back with your headphones. In Troy Smith's opinion, "we realized millennials are coming to the tasting rooms always expecting a change up, something new all the time and the goal for today's breweries. You'll see evolving taps, and at 980, our old Vista facility, you'll see small pilot batches, and one-off styles being brewed all the time."

Tom Vogel's involvement in the brewing industry leads to many valuable overviews on brewing. "We wanted to make beer palatable to everybody. So, we have the smoother beers, the milk stouts, honeys, saisons, for all entry level with many session-styled fresh drinkable flavors. We feature our IPAs, and stouts, yet the entry level beers add more delicate flavors." As Tom's wife would say, "It's fabulous." Or, customers say, "They're all fabulous." Then, there's the hop aroma, the grapefruit flavors, the honey overtones to delight the palate. "I just say, Man, great beer!"

BNS Brewing & Distilling Co.

East County San Diego
10960 Wetlands Ave. Suite 101
Santee, CA 92071
619-956-0952
www.BNSBrewing.com

Gene Chaffin, Facilitator
Dan Jenson, Head Brewer

Through the swinging patio gate, strolling into BNS Brewing and Distilling Company's massive 12,000 sq. ft. warehouse reveals the charm of a Western frontier barroom complimented by corresponding West Coast style beer and distilled spirits. Opened June 2013, "Beer and Spirits," owner Gene Chaffin points out the name simply translates to BNS. It was a time Gene recalls, "Santee had only one other brewery, and coastline breweries are nearly 20 miles away. We are fortunate enough having Coronado's former head brewer, Dan Jensen as our master brewer. He's putting our beer on the map at the GABF, winning two golds with one for an IPA, another for our Red Ale and adding on a silver medal for our Stout." Gene, a long time San Diego general and electrical contractor admits, "I know little about brewing beer, but the opportunity opened for us constructing a brewing facility for Coronado Brewing Company by Mission Bay. We completed their brand new 20,000 sq. ft. headquarters in 2012. At the time, I was working at this very brewery and distillery site completing construction for the original owners." As Gene explains, "I finished the work, but there was difficultly paying off the brewery when it fell into default. I decided it would be a great potential retiring from contracting and taking over the ownership, so I acquire it." And, BNS Brewing & Distilling has become a masterwork of Gene's ingenuity ever since.

There's an unusual configuration with a distillery housed in a brewery which by law must be separated with individual entries. At BNS, highlighting the entry with a tall red facade barn and door inside the brewery leads to tastings of freshly distilled vodkas, whiskeys, rum, gin, bourbon, and moonshine produced in-house. Handcrafted distilled products are headed by Blake Heffernan, also a specialty brewer and distiller. "BNS has opened one of the only distilleries allowed inside a brewery," as Gene describes, "and we began distilling vodka.

When it's made not quite as pure qualifying it as vodka, then it's known as a lesser grade called moonshine. We have mixed tasters to sample, some with added coffee or fruits, or we'll even make apple tasting moonshine. Bourbon has to be 51% corn to make it a straight bourbon, then is aged in virgin charred barrels for two years. Also, there are local wineries we are distilling batches of wines for making brandy. The San Pasquale Winery collaboration under way is put away into charred oak barrels, up to three years. Gene plans to manufacture whiskeys beginning with a beer recipe at 10% abv, "I call grog, because it's made from fermented grain blends. Then, we distill it taking all the alcohol off and barrel-age the final results." The new 50-gallon still by a Kentucky manufacturer carries the right pedigree for finely distilled spirits, up to 150-proof.

BNS participates supporting community events and fundraisers. The brewery venue is open for weddings, retirements, baby showers, and even a monthly 5-hour Cornhole contest set up by a traveling company. Every Friday and Saturday, there live bands and songwriters. Santee invites BNS to attend their street fairs and annual events at the golf course, near East Lake. "We are a smaller nano-brewery making about 1,500 barrels a year yet Costco came to us, and we have picked up distribution contracts in Las Vegas, and we're working on Arizona. We have made strides reaching a growing market," Gene cites regarding the future, "and we'll self-distribute 60-70 deliveries to tap rooms locally." BNS simply, the purity making beer with no extracts and real ingredients with handmade preparation has brought forward the best possible quality in San Diego.

BOLT BREWERY

8179 Center St.
La Mesa, CA 91942

Little Italy Brew House Tasting Room
1971 India Street
San Diego, CA 92102
www.boltbrewery.com
619-303-7837

Clint Stromberg / Molly Rust Co-owners
Chris Angel, Head Brewer
Josh Ferracioli, Brewer

In 1987, San Diego's first ever craft brewery was tucked away in a quonset hut during a brief, but spectacular opening. The original Bolt Brewery brought together Clint Stromberg, an eager apprentice at the age of 19, and master brewer, Paul Holborn's move to North County's Fallbrook avocado farming region. They singlehandedly set in motion an era's legacy well before any other brewery past the days of post-prohibition in San Diego. Incessant demand had the brewery running at full speed, and eventually required more than simple upgrades. After a few years, Clint left San Diego to explore the traditions of Europe's great brewing history traveling into the eastern block hills of Hungary. There, Clint fabricated his fabled handmade 10-barrel copper brewing system

for a client in Budapest, in 1995. Those copper clad kettles built in Hungary, serendipitously followed him home creating a remarkable reunion. After finding the equipment for sale, he acquired the brewing kettles 30 years later, helping to reopen Bolt Brewery with his own custom equipment epitomizing Bolt's great up-to-date beer. The brewing facility maintains production up to 2,000 barrels of beer annually. Bolt Brewing's "deja vu" going forward has leapt into a latest quonset brew hut, adjacent to Bolt Brewery's beer garden and tap room in La Mesa, just east of San Diego metro. Previously in 1990, Clint made plans redeveloping the old Mission Brewery Plaza building near the airport, bringing back to life the historical facility, only disappointed by the city's planners unpreparedness dealing with brewery regulations. Then, in 2010 he successfully established Five Points Brewery in the Mission Brewery Plaza, brewing beer and joining the huge demand for San Diego craft beer. The journey led with partner Molly Rust, and the current Bolt Brewery in 2014. Located today in a former industrial area once an industrial scrapyard, the property's new setting presents a garden bar and taps next to a familiar quonset housing Clint's vintage handmade copper brewing kettles. Bolt Brewing opened a second tasting room on India St. in Little Italy, just above San Diego's harbor.

Currently rotating 25 beers through their 20 taps at each location. The breweries offer table seating, food, and weekend entertainment. Stromberg along with his team of brewers, Chris Angel, Josh Ferracioli, and Nick Pankow bring traditional session ales and lagers ranging from pilsner, pale ales, IPAs, and stouts. More importantly, Bolt remains a legendary part of San Diego's craft genesis. Bolt Brewery's locations take part in today's back to the future craft establishing San Diego traditional beer recipes. The downtown tasting room and restaurant serves lunches, dinners, and daily specials, with fresh craft beer flowing once again at the Bolt Brewery taps.

Bolt Brewery opened before all other SD craft breweries in 1987, in Fallbrook. Today, Bolt Brewery's quonset hut theme has an open air bar, set squarely in La Mesa's industrial zone.

BNS's outlying Santee location stays true to Old West branding. Just southeast of San Diego's metro area, they produce both great beer and distilled spirits made to perfection in one building.

Citizens Brewers owner, Judd McGhee, guides each student brewer through the process for brewing a perfect keg of craft beer of most any style craft beer.

In the center of Oceanside's busy Mission Street business district near the Pacific Ocean, Booze Brothers invite visitors to a new tasting room for enjoying their craft directly from the source.

BOOZE BROTHERS BREWING CO.

2545 Progress St. Suite D
Vista, CA 92081
760-295-0217

Oceanside Tasting Room
606 Mission Ave.
Oceanside, CA 92054
www.boozebros.com

Dave Firth, Owner   Kris Anacleto, General Manager
Donny Firth, Owner / Master Brewer Maurey Fletcher, Head Brewer

In 2013, North County's team Donny and Dave Firth were nicknamed the Booze Brothers early on. As brothers, they accumulated 5 years' home brewing experience and built a local enterprise overtaking their garage after setting up a mixture of equipment. Leaving a scarcity of seating for increasing numbers of their friends and enthusiasts each weekend, the time had come considering a brewing business. Dave's pool business had tanked and inspired an upgrade, at the same time the popularity of craft brewers took off in their hometown of Vista. Having a first hand look at local brewing success, the timing couldn't of been better starting their own brewery. Locating equipment for a professional brewery came a priority of help from other brewers, adding to a collection of their own. A brewing facility, tasting room and event facility, Booze Brothers Brewing Co.'s features skillfully crafted beer, unique and diversified for an abundance of exploration. The Booze Brothers initially moved into a suite of industrial spaces converting the brew house into a polished taproom with a comfortable patio and event area. In 2019, Booze Brothers Specialty Stout, Black Sunshine won a Gold Medal at the San Diego International Beer Festival.

Speaking about reaching people about beer, Mr. Manager at the brewery, Kris Anacleto relates, "any normal day we have 15 beers on tap, and about a dozen are our staple core beers. Generally, there are three beers rotated presenting entirely new recipes. And on Mondays, we're opened with the back bar for 10 uniquely styled featured one-off beer for individual tastings. It has become a

great stopping off spot for sampling freshness, as well as finding opinionated conversations about beer found nowhere else."

Maurey, Head Brewer had spent his past career at the Oceanside's Hydro-Brew home brew shop and became a mead maker at Golden Coast Mead, locally in Oceanside. His talents have given rise to a new perspective about brewing new beer at Booze Brothers. As Kris explained, "Breweries cannot legally sell wine, but we do have unique types of braggot, a hybrid of mead and ale. The brewery's core line up of beer begins with a consistent favorite Old Granddaddy IIPA, that's a double IPA at 8.2% abv. Penny Blonde has a smooth summery crisp, lightly hopped flavors. Honey Bloom carries hints of Scottish heather. Good Guy Pale Ale meets the West Coast standard with tasty Cascade, Belma and Columbus hops. There's a lighter single hop Crow Jane IPA. Snow Blind and Cherry Blind Wit are stronger Belgian Wit beer. Other choices include Easy Rider Brown, Buena Vista IPA, and Sunup Stout, each with increasing abv percentages. A barrel-aging program has developed creating cellared sour ales and blonds. A recent development of the brewery's new event space suite is open to accommodate private parties and weddings. The team has doubled the size of the brewing area, upgrading their existing 10-barrel system modifying and increasing it's busy production schedule for local distribution. Expanding the brewery's output from its opening in 2013, the Booze Brothers are gaining notice from the craft beer scene in San Diego, as well as filling the brewery with old friends seeking the legendary "underground garage beers" of Dave and Donny Firth.

CITIZEN BREWERS

5837 Mission Gorge Rd. Ste. A
San Diego, CA 92120
760-587-7989
www.citizenbrewers.com

Judd McGhee, Owner / Brewer

Downtown San Diego's Citizens Brewers presents a common sense approach to demystifying the art of making your own beer. Catering to craft beer enthusiasts in pursuit of the best way to begin brewing, what's better than having your own personal mentor? Citizens Brewers does an amazing job for anyone wanting to enjoy an introduction to professional brewing equipment and take the first steps creating a craft beer on their own. You are guided through each step using scratch ingredients, at the same time avoiding equipment costs or the space taken in your garage or backyard. It's a service available from Judd McGhee at Citizens Brewers for brewing your own recipe, or any of the 12 house beer styles with his guidelines and suggestions. The results yield about six cases, one 50-liter keg, or around 72, 22-ounce bottles. You even can add your own artistic design and print out self-adhering labels at the brewery. It's for anyone without prior knowledge about brewing but some experience may help. If you are working up idea for a brewing recipe, or just ready to experience running real brewing equipment, Citizen Brewers solves the problem.

Judd McGhee launched the unique brewing system in November 2015, capturing the daily fervor for craft beer in a novel way. He opened his new business to encourage home brewers interested in making their own craft beer using the benefits of specialized equipment at Citizen Brewers. You will find full attention is paid to filtering water using reverse osmosis, copper clad brew kettles with steam jackets and temperature controlled fermentation at the brewery. Beginning with RO, water may be tailored by deciding on the ionic composition attributed to each style of beer. The choice using the right water enhances flavors especially when brewing delicate lighter colors and will result in increased crispness in taste. There are a dozen choice house recipes brewers may select at Citizen Brewers and choose the correct yeast, malt, hops, or adjunct flavor ingredients may be supplied either by individuals in training or directly from Judd's own stockpile. The initial brewing time varies from two to four hours for the first process. Then within six weeks, each brewer returns another two hours finishing off the bottling of their fresh brew. Judd supplies keg rentals and bottles when needed at the brewery. Judd explains, "Typically it's people coming to Citizen's Brewery that love beer but haven't tried home brewing, but then there are a few who bring in their own recipes and methods. I'm more a guide than a mentor being I want people to be empowered and give them the reins revealing the process and becoming involved."

It will take about four to six weeks between brewing and bottling to make a West Coast IPA adding in dry hopping for bitterness. There's a recipe at the brewery for nearly for any master craft style including Double IPA, India Pale Lager, Kölsch, American Amber Ale, Bavarian Hefeweisen, Pale Ale, Mosaic Wheat Ale, Belgian Farmhouse Saison, Northern English Brown, Irish Stout, and Robust Porter. Judd sums

Citizens Brewery supplies everything to assist first time and seasoned home brewers.

it up, "Citizen Brewers is a place for people to come if they're interested in brewing their own beer and looking for a streamlined guided process. I provide a space not unlike a commercial kitchen but geared towards brewing. I offer up utilities and equipment to produce beer and other carbonated beverages, and whether this is your first time or hundredth time brewing, we want this to be a personalized, unforgettable experience."

CORONADO BREWING COMPANY

Main Brewery and Tasting Room
1205 Knoxville St.
San Diego, CA 92110
619-275-6700

Original Brewpub
170 Orange Ave.
Coronado, CA 92118
619-437-4452

Restaurant and Tasting Room
875 Seacoast Dr.
Imperial Beach, CA 91932
619-423-4900
www.coronadobrewing.com

Ron & Rick Chapman, founders of Coronado Brewing Company.

Established in 1996, Coronado Brewing Company remains the first and only brewery on Coronado Island. Brothers, Rick and Ron Chapman were pioneers of craft brewing's newest generation gathered along California's southern coastal shores. The brewery's getaway beach town brewpub has been a contribution as the perfect place for friends enjoying great beer and a good meal in a laid-back atmosphere. Coronado Brewing became the fifth craft brewery in San Diego, and their brewing continues to impart a personal expression of the brothers' finely handcrafted beer at the cutting edge of craft.

Fast forward to the increasing demands of production for their fresh beer in 2012, and the decision for Coronado Brewery relocating the headquarters to today's Knoxville production facility and tasting room, at the edge of San Diego's Mission Bay. Open to the public daily, the brewery's tasting room has become the source of freshly made Coronado craft beer, barrel-aged beer and sours, while featuring full view of brewery operations in action. In 2014, the owners dedicated a third venue in Imperial Beach, the newest Coronado

Brewing tasting room location, with a farm fresh restaurant specializing in quick service appetizers, salads, tacos & wraps, great beer pairings, beer to go, crowlers and growler fills. A few miles from the Mexican border, the new location fulfills the family's vision of operating a community business within their own neighborhood. Coronado Brewing celebrated its 24th Anniversary in 2020, culminating with a celebration at the Knoxville brewery. Melody Crisp, a certified Beer Cicerone and BCJP Judge, describes the company's moving along a circuitous path, "by opening the new location, the owners Ron and Rick will go back to their own hometown in Imperial Beach. The latest project includes a 15,000 square foot space, a smaller 7-barrel brewing system, and full service restaurant. San Diego's craft scene had just begun expansion to the south bay, and we're very happy about bringing a whole other group of people to knowing about Coronado Brewing Company and the craft beer movement."

Coronado Brewing earned what's regarded as the highest achievements in the craft beer universe receiving the World Beer Cup's 2014 'Champion Best Mid-Sized Brewery' & 'Mid-Sized Brewing Company Brewer of the Year.' That same year, the brewery brought home a Gold Medal honoring their Islander IPA, a flagship American-style strong; as well as, a Silver Medal for a barley wine style, Old Scallywag. Coronado's famed flavors are always related to the esoteric origins of brewing styles in varying degrees of hops and malts. The brewery consistently is known for its IPAs, yet offers a wide range of beer styles. Melody describes the line of Coronado's core beer as all inclusive and ever expanding.

"Our brewmaster is a huge fan of classic beer following the traditional rules. It's a solid foundation knowing how to break them, as well." The majority of Coronado's styles are sold in recyclable cans and with nine favorite core beers, Melody called attention to two recently released, Bronze Medal winner at the 2017 San Diego International Beer Festival in Del Mar. "Coronado's Seacoast Pilsner, a session beer measuring 4.9% abv, and 18 ibu, an ideal thirst quenching beer is meant for perfect enjoyment during the heat of a southern coastal day. Recent 2019 competitive awards at the Great American Beer Festival, Denver,

In view of the tap and tasting room, Coronado Brewing's main brewing facility and operations is located at the Knoxville Street near Mission Bay, not far from downtown San Diego.

Co. brought home a Gold Medal for an American-Style Amber / Mermaid's Red Ale, and a Silver Medal for their Never Better Imperial India Pale Ale. Other awards from the San Diego International Beer Festival earned a Silver Medal for Coronado's Freebooter Barleywine Ale, and a Bronze Medal to their American-Style India Pale Ale, Weekend Vibes IPA, a hop-forward Mosaic, Citra and Simcoe blend.

The Knoxville Brewery's tasting room supplies customers' take-home crowlers, that are practical recyclable 32 oz. cans, sealed tightly for lasting freshness and right from the brewery tap. The Coronado Brewing Collection highlights favorite classic barrel-aged bottled and draft releases. A limited release introduced in 2016, a popular hazy IPA was first brewed on the island and named North Island IPA. It became so in demand the beer was added to

the seasonal program. It's a 7.5% abv, juicy IPA at 40 ibu and carries notes of citrus aromas and hop flavors without a hard bitterness. Salty Crew Blonde Ale, is the perfect crisp, versatile and refreshing boat beer that goes where no glass can. Throw in a lime, make it bloody or spice the rim for a classic twist. "We definitely see our flagship core beer and more exotic styles in our portfolio representing the elements of discovery and diversity of craft beer in San Diego, it's often the way we bring attention to our newer styles." The latest buzz for Coronado Brewing beer enthusiasts exemplifies "Stay Coastal", and homage to a dedication towards protecting our natural resources and the coastline waters enveloping the island. Also, it becomes clear to visitors new to Coronado, it's is not only the best choice of excellent San Diego craft beer, but a picture perfect destination island getaway to enjoy!

SDIBF Bronze Medal winnerv American-Style India Pale Ale, Weekend Vibes IPA

The original landmark brewpub of the Coronado Brewing Company at 170 Orange Ave., on Coronado Island. (Courtesy of Coronado Brewing Company)

A flight of tasters at Coronado's main brewery at the Knoxville Tasting Room provides a comparison of craft flavors and styles of their premium draft beers.

Local North County brewers Dave & Donny Firth began Booze Brothers Brewery in Vista. The new tasting room in Oceanside brings their craft beer to a busy marketplace on Mission Ave.

Belching Beaver's North County fresh IPAs and a variety of specialty brews are available in Ocean Beach's Newport Ave. district.

Culver Beer Co.

2719 Loker Ave. Ste D
Carlsbad, CA 92010
760-814-2355
www.culverbeer.com

Ben Fairweather, owner / brewer
Mike Stevenson, owner / head brewer

Mike and Ben enjoy a brief break at the brewery.

"I was working professionally in the industry and Ben was homebrewing. We found out Carlsbad had changed over its municipal code and was going to start allowing small breweries applications in the industrial zone, and we wanted to be the first one through." Mike Stevenson

Culver Beer Co.'s brewery tasting room offers an inviting escape either on the way, or back from your favorite Carlsbad beach resort. It's known for adventurous inventive craft beers and located just off Palomar Airport Road, near Melrose. North County San Diego natives, Ben Fairweather and Mike Stevenson had planned on craft brewing careers and recognized their mutual interests were developing over years. Attending Coachella Festival, they nailed down a partnership and celebrated a Grand Opening anniversary on June 30th, 2016. Culver Beer Co. broke into the scene soon after with a Bronze Medal at the San Diego International Beer Festival in 2017 for Tiger Ride, a Belgian Pale Ale; and in 2018, earned another Bronze for Daily Routine, a Bold Stout.

Exploring great beer is highlighted by brilliant cartoonist, colorist, and branding artist, Spencer Ramsey @yesmarble and his work with the brewery. A long time friend involved primarily with skateboarding art, includes amazing handdrawn label designs, as well as colorful M.C. Escheresque style renderings. Both Ben and Mike's alliance with Spencer's whimsical characters accurately portrays their beer's characteristic styles and brand names. New millennium imagery speaks loudly to the brewery's business model. "It is an artistic direction and definitely helps shape the brand into something reflecting our attitude and personalities. Spencer has given life to our brand which is quite possibly one of the most important parts to opening a brewery... besides great beer, of course!"

As their business grows, Culver Beer's tasting room is popular for friendly community meetups, and often filled with repeat customers. The tasting room serves choices of craft beers ranging from Belgians, Lagers, Fruited, Ales, Stouts, Porters to Barrel Aged Sours, served from as many as 18 taps. Sampling Culver craft beer inside their hand-crafted tasting room works well for the team's rich array of flavors. Above the bar, the beer taps are color-coded in groups with corresponding beer styles with identifying names to what's available. IPA's color is green, Irish and Amaretto ales are redish brown, Porters and Strongs are brown, yellow for Blondes and black for Stouts.

Mike uses his extensive knowledge from an early apprenticeship with European brewers in northwest Germany, and the Italian island of Sardinia, as well as a short stint of employment at White Labs International headquarters, a well known San Diego brewer and yeast provider. The team brings all their skills together at the brewery, and as Mike reminisces, "traveling always has been a big part of my life. My mom is a flight attendant, and we would take quite a few trips growing up. When I had graduated college I was serving tables and looking for an experience. I e-mailed most family owned breweries in Germany and found a perfect fit near Cologne working in a brewpub/bed and breakfast. It was a great adventure, and a perfect resume boost getting me in the local industry. I am very thankful for my time out there."

Locally Toasted Delicatessen adds to Culver Beer's tasting room, offering quality sandwiches to pair with delicious beers.

Indian Joe's Brewing has expanded over the years under Max Moran's brewing acuity, and main facility is right off the Hop Highway 78, in San Marcos.

A wall compares hundreds of early brews from the industry in a collection on display in San Marcos, at Rip Current Brewing.

DOS DESPERADOS BREWERY

1241 Linda Vista Dr.
San Marcos, CA 92078
Phone: 760-566-6209
www.dosdesperadosbrew.com

Steve & Dora Munson, Co-owners
Hayden Weir, Brewer

With nearly 20 years home brewing success, Steve Munson decided the right time had come to set up a drinking hole in San Marcos, and Dos Desperados Brewing opened their doors in 2014. It's been a family affair everyday, and each week one of the Munson family may be seen running the tap room. Steve's ideal had been aimed at meeting customers after retiring several years ago from the corporate world. "It's the experience of different beer, friends and family that got me into home brewing," Steve explains. He developed his own in-house recipe ideas to optimal refinement, and several beers have earned reputations at the San Diego International Beer Festival. In 2015, a Bronze Medal was awarded for the Unique Ingredient Beer class, featuring his Scotch Bonnet Imperial Stout. The following year brought home two Silver Medal awards and included Maniac Imperial Stout, and Habeerneros IPA.

After a visitor from a German brewing family stopped by Steve's tap room and commented they'd not found on the menu a hefeweizen or true wheat beer; they left Steve their family's recipe, and it's become a core beer at Dos Desperados. It's called El Hefe, and as light and refreshing as it's cousin in Europe. Matched only by a Kölsch style at the brewery, Blonde Kölsch, another saloon favorite

seller. It was awarded a Gold
Medal in Del Mar at the San Diego
International Beer Festival in 2017,
and a traditional German craft
beer, it is light and crispy with a
hinted aroma of grape, at 4.8% abv
and 20 ibu.

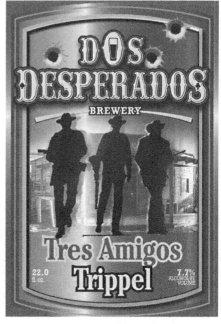

Dos Desperados has brought
frequent satisfaction to Steve as
a brewer. Pushing the bar much
higher, the brewery's Pancho Villa
Double IPA is the type that might
of induced a gunfight back in the
day at 9.2% abv and 98 ibu. And,
it's triple dry-hopped, exuding a
malty sweetness and fruity aroma.
Also, Gunsmoke Habeerneros
Scottish is winner of Channel
6's Best Beer in San Diego, during Spring 2015. With seasonal fruits and
veggies grown throughout San Diego's countryside, choices for blood oranges,
pumpkins, and Steve's specialty, habaneros peppers are available locally and
contribute to each beer's inspiration.

Top off a visit at the saloon with the red Ruff Ryeder IPA Ale, Jailbreak IPA,
or Most Wanted Citrus IPA, all tasteful specialties at Dos Desperados Brewing.
Open every day of the week, Steve comments, "You must differentiate yourself
a little bit and number one is – the beer has to be really good, and it has to
be a really good experience. We had as many at eight IPAs on tap during the
summer months, but by this spring we'll have just four or five only because it's a
customer driven business. We have favorite local customers, and we sell growlers
and kegs mainly in California. We make session beer around a 4.8% abv, and we
try to listen to what customers prefer in color, taste, and hops."

Located off the Los Posas exit on Hop Highway State 78, where the brewery
faces the freeway and just a short ride down the trail. So, dust off your boots and
mosey on into the toughest and tastiest brewery in town and bring a friend to
enjoy an incredible beer at the saloon's watering hole, pardner!

DUCK FOOT BREWING COMPANY

8920 Kenamar Dr. Ste 210
San Diego, CA 92121
858-433-7916
www.duckfootbeer.com

Matt DelVecchio, Head Quack
Brett Goldstock, Chief Fermentation Officer

When in Miramar, "If it looks like a duck and quacks like a duck," then you know you're probably drinking a fine ale at Duck Foot Brewery. Located under the shadow of the landmark Innovation Center Pyramid on Kenamar Road, the brewery has served quality gluten-reduced ales since June 2015. Head Quack, Matt DelVecchio began home brewing while living in New York City. After leaving a cozy position in New York's financial realm, the story became an overnight reality and success story. His own experience lead him to believe gluten-free beer could bring a strong concept for brewing within the San Diego craft industry. Moving west, his mild manner and occasional malt mustache faced the reality of celiac disease, a health issue created from the gluten content in most grains. With his wife Katie, they planned on settling in Encinitas and starting a family, and Matt began brewing professionally making gluten-reduced beer establishing Duck Foot Brewing Company. The Miramar tasting room provides a comfortable setting suited for enjoying zestful refreshing beer any day of the week.

Duck Foot Brewery's core line up concentrates on pleasing all palettes. West Coast style ales are both hoppy and bitter with a touch of biscuity, bready malt sweetness, and perhaps a bit on the sour side. All Duck Foot beer uses a special enzyme removing nearly all traces of gluten from the beer. Brett Goldstock, Matt's brewing partner and Chief Fermentation Officer moved from New York joining the San Diego-based QUAFF club and is a devoted practitioner over 20 years brewing beer, mead, and cider. Brett enters brewing competitions nationally and also actively judges beer competitions.

His certification as a BJCP National Beer Judge, as well as a Mead Judge adds integrity and quality to each and every Duck Foot beer. At 2017's San Diego International Beer Festival in Del Mar, two Gold Medals added to the brewery's growing reputation. Black Leprechaun, a Specialty Stout, and London Calling, a Porter brought the highest honors. At 2019's festival, Duck Foot earned a Silver Medal, and Gold in 2018 for Redrum Wood & Barrel Aged; and a Silver Medal for the unique Coconut Contender IPA. There's a variety of appealing choices at the brewery tasting room. Duckzilla Double White IPA, a hybrid of a White Ale and West Coast IPA, and Duckzilla Double IPA offers a citrus bomb of Centennial, Cascade and Citra hops adding only real grapefruit juice zest and absolutely no extracts! A dark Choco Nut Lust, a full-bodied Chocolate Hazelnut Porter malt forward flavor never misleads one's senses for a strong balance of molasses, caramel, brown sugar, dark chocolate, coconut, and added cocoa nibs with real chopped hazelnuts. A small amount of Cascade hops adds balance creating less bitterness and malt sweetness. The Contender West Coast-style IPA has a light and refreshing big flavor and aroma at 6.5% abv. Once fermentation is completed, a generous blast of Simcoe hops is dry hopped for citrusy pine aromas and flavors. RoJoe Gringo Red Ale reflects appealing crimson colors comes using several red beer styles in combination carrying a malt forward flavor. The Looker - the Duck Foot classic American Blonde Ale is a combination of pale and caramelized malts brewed into a light refreshing flavor. Duck Foot distributes throughout stores and pubs in San Diego and Los Angeles. The brewery commitment opening the market to less gluten-heavy brews adds more value to the consumer's enjoyment of craft beer!

EBULLITION BREW WORKS

2449 Cades Way
Vista, CA
760-842-1046
www.ebullitionbrew.com

Ebullition Brew Works & Gastronomy
2628 Gateway Rd. E-135
Carlsbad, CA 92009
442-282-2837

Jesse Richardson, Owner / Brewer
Erik Dyrr, Owner / Brewer
Jan Buncher, Co-owner
Mike Reidy, Brewer

A trip into the heart of Vista's brewery warehouses greets visitors to the tap room of one of the newest 10-barrel craft breweries named after beer's cheerful feeling of ebullience. The meaning of ebullition eludes to an outpouring springing from life; but co-owner, Jesse Richardson relates it technically "to a brewing term encompassing the process of beer wort at its peak boiling point, as well as the bursting of energy, passion, and emotion." Ebullition Brew Works takes off under the combined spirit of three partners including Jesse, his cousin Erik Dyrr and associate Jan Buncher. "We were surrounded by the brewery buzz of 2009 having Lost Abbey, Stone and Iron Fist right nearby. We always shared our home brewed beer with friends who enjoyed our samples. We decided on buying a 3-barrel system Mother Earth home brewing kit and realized we could start a business on the side in just 800 square feet. Jesse recalls, "I was involved in the corporate world of marketing and getting married. By then, North County breweries were popping up including Aztec, Toolbox and Belching Beaver. Green Flash vacated their first home in Vista after huge growth, and we decided to check out the warehouse. It lit a fire to our imagination starting our brewery and all we talked about. Amanda Cole, Jesse's wife worked at Stone brewing for several years and inside invitations came to attend events. Meeting Mitch Steele, a pioneer brewer developing Stone's earliest brews, and Rick Blankemeier, who worked quality control at Stone Brewing and Modern Times Brewing, helped bring home the potential of opening a small successful brewing company of their own. After years of home brewing, we decided to write a business plan."

Erik completed a search for buildings finding Vista a preferred choice for breweries. He explains, "The building came to us after Jan mentioned his brother-in-law happened to own the very building we're in today. After we checked out the size, open area, and how it fit, everything came together within the 4,000 sq ft., an exact size we had in mind. Working on the interior of the tasting room, the crew created an intricate design of a giant overhead exposed beam lattice above the tasting room bar. The beams represent over-the-top craftsmanship matched by the brewery's handcrafted polished bar, earthy wood paneling, and great beer. Abundant seating in the brewery offers wireless device-friendly AC charging stations finishing off the upscale design. Piloting Ebullition's first brews, veteran brewmaster Mike Reidy entered the role as professional brewer from San Diego's Quaff, and as a long time member of the Society of Barley Engineers, San Diego's best home brewer communities. Joining the Ebullition team early in 2017, Mike brought the brewery up to full running speed for the Grand Opening in October. "Our vision offers an experience for each person trying something new in the tasting room. Mike was the perfect choice as brewer." Jesse adds, "we decided our best chance for growth would be to skip the smaller nano-brewery by installing a 10-barrel brewing system from the advice of PBST, Pacific Brewery Systems. So, we were able to get the perfect equipment fitting our budget." Open on Wednesdays through Sundays, using the extended hours provided by the city regulations of Vista, the team plans on upbeat live entertainment at the brewery. "We feel we have a treasure in the rough, a place that is not hard to find but takes a little looking," Jesse furthered the idea, "as Mike likes to say, from Sycamore make a right on Grand, a right on Cades and right-on beer!"

GROUNDSWELL BREWING COMPANY

Grantville Tasting Room
6304 Riverdale St.
San Diego, CA 92120
619-795-BEER
www.groundswellbrewing.com

Brewery and Tasting Room
10151 Prospect Ave.
Santee, CA 92071
619-749-9123

Kevin Rhodes, President / Head Brewer
Christianne Penunuri, Marketing / Events

Kevin Rhodes deliberated on finding a brewing name defining "Community". He could foresee making great beer and contributing as part of the community of craft brewers in San Diego. From the conversations at

home, one brought up "Groundswell," and it gained instant approval of friends
and family setting in motion the launch of Groundswell Brewing Company
in early 2013. Opening his first nano-brewery in San Diego's Mission Valley
region called Grantville, Kevin emphasized the decision for the brewery's name,
"had come from an idea of a grass roots movement in the community and
helping people move their cause along. We wanted to begin with a very small
brewery and create wide acceptance and success as the direction we wanted to
go." Groundswell Brewing became a reality springing from Kevin's favorite
passion of 25 years home brewing. The brewery had turned into a perfect
downtown destination, also an ideal place for the collection of accumulated
brewing equipment he owned. Kevin also purchased a professional one-barrel

commercial brewing system for working up his pilot recipes. When it comes to the beer, Kevin qualifies, "we brew what we call our sunshine beers. Our beer is great in a can and near the pool, even complimenting many types of recreation. Our IPAs aren't over the top bitter and out in the sun you'll still maintain energy. Our groove is making good tasting beer. We do not try to redefine beer, we're more in the middle and not hard edged. Now our newest brewery facility gives us some latitude to experiment and begin barrel-aging beer sours and tarts." During 2016-2017's tidal wave of brewery grand openings, Kevin began expanding his operations in January 2017 establishing a new southern warehouse destination in Santee, CA. This formidable facility has eight 60-barrel fermenters with a 30-barrel system running a smooth flowing supply to his customers of Groundswell's best beer. And, the new brewery wing produces beer fulfilling Groundswell's larger role with a larger plan as Kevin explains, "we have fruit sours in rotation, and we'll be making a fruit IPA in the future. Soon, we'll be brewing a whole new menu of styles."

Nearby, Stehly Farms Organics in Valley Center grows the types of fruit needed to enhance beer flavor and finding the most natural ingredients is an necessary choice for Groundswell Brewing. Wary of bacteria contaminating the beer, the farm supplies a fruit puree perfect as a beer adjunct. "We can brew about 30 times a month, but we're not close to that right now. We'll also be working as a facility for other brewers needing to keep up with demand. We have a good relationships with brewers, and we'll treat their beer just like our own making it according to their schedules to deliver fresh beer without it sitting around." Kevin's background began in the hospitality business, and he had been a dedicated restaurateur over 20 years. "The only way being successful at business is treating everyone at the highest level with no shortcuts, and that's a key to great hospitality. I started teaching hospitality classes at the San Diego Art Institute in Mission Valley, and my interests took a turn after I took over a course on wine education and pairings. Then as a home brewer, we were just at the beginning of beer pairings becoming recognized. I gained my certification with the Wine & Spirits Education Trust and began thinking from the food side how to brew craft beer using a culinary angle - it's about balance and more flavors."

Success at 2018's San Diego International Beer Festival brought a Gold Medal for Groundswell's American Style Brown Ale, Piloncillo Brown, as well as a Bronze for Your Mama's Boy. A friendly tasting room beertender guides you through the latest Groundswell choices. Prevailing seasonal beers may include several interesting styles and as Kevin explains, "The Full Ginger Saison featuring Belgian yeast imparts a fruity tartness adding aromas to the nose from a dry hop of ginger root. Pogue Mahone is a hybrid style based off the once popular ESB (Extra Special Bitter.) It's malt forward hints of caramel, toffee, and cherry, makes it lighter in bitterness than its English-born relative, and there are specialty malts providing a deep red appearance fitting it's Irish name." Other beers include, "our Mocha Milk Stout, a nutty, medium-bodied brew with two-row malt, cocoa nibs, and local cold brew coffee imparting a chocolate coffee bitterness making an easy drinking full-flavored stout. Our Red IPA, brewed with Jarrylo and Simcoe hops, has an aroma of fruity spice, pine, and hints of pear sweet on the palette with a lingering hop bitterness distinctive of West Coast IPA's. Another, Groundswell Hefeweizen, is a true Bavarian Hefeweizen featuring more than 50% wheat malt achieving a full-bodied crisp light wheat beer low in bitterness and hop aroma. There's a sweet taste and hazy appearance helping make this easy drinking beer a favorite for a full range of beer drinkers. The Mango Tart is the first in the Groundswell Sour Suite, and it's a kettle-soured beer not overly done. There's a tart and balanced rich mango aroma and flavor but a mellow finish that cleanses the palate." Although San Diego is famous for its super aggressive hoppy beer, the goal contrasts Groundswell's commitment to a consistency in serving delicate flavors. Kevin's brewing ethics insists on, "controlling our own brewing destiny with the goal of serving a thirsty world."

INDIAN JOE BREWING

2123 Industrial Court
Vista, CA 92081
760-295-3945
www.indianjoebrewing.com

Max Moran, President
Geri Lawson, Vice-President

If you're traveling along the Hop Highway 78, you'll not want to miss visiting Indian Joe Brewing in Vista, North County San Diego. If you've not been at the brewery yet, a tasting room experience awaits an entire range of beer flavors. After meeting Max Moran, "Chief of Them All", you'll find there's a choice from hundreds of recipes featuring 20-30 beers always on tap. There are beer styles to sample a flight of eight, as one option. Craft beer is organized on a style sheet with descriptions and details. Additionally, there are aged sours fermented in wooden barrels requiring six-months to over a year to maturity. There's even a freshly brewed natural sassafras root beer with a tall head and other choices for non-alcoholic beverages, each beyond one's imagination.

The recent success of Indian Joe's for the IJB Imperial Oatmeal Stout won a Gold Medal; and a Smoked Beer, Ham for the Holidays, won a Bronze Medal at the 2019 San Diego International Beer Festival. Their American Style Amber/ Red Ale brought home a Bronze Medal at 2018's festival, following in 2017, a Bronze Medal for their awesome Pineapple Passionfruit Gose, a German-style Weiss. Max insists successful brewing is the result of several consistent goals. "One thing at Indian Joe's, we use 100% real fruit in our beer. We'll source out our honey from a family run business, Temecula Valley Honey Co. and use a local organic ranch, Stehly Farms in Valley Center. The freshest harvested crops include wonderful blueberries, raspberries and blackberries, even citrus, and avocados. Sometimes, there are 600 to 800 lbs. of fruit added to a 30-barrel batch. I have a friend visiting from the Lakota Nation who brings their mountain sage in trade for our root beer brewed with fresh sassafras and agave sweetener for non-drinkers and designated drivers. Luiseño Red Ale is styled from my own tribe of San Luis Rey, Pechanga, Pala, Pauma, and Rincon natives from the Mt. Palomar area. We'll use herbs like white sage, or Hummingbird sage carefully prepared for our beer. We consider ourselves innovators

Max often spends up to 19 hours a day running the 15-bbl system at Indian Joes Brewing, using proprietary recipes developed over 20 years.

formulating our own recipes, never following anyone else."

Max's family roots date to Spanish Alta California at Mission San Luis Rey where as servants his forebears tended grape vines. His great-great maternal grandparents, Honorato and Refugia Garcia were the servants at Rancho Guajome and Rancho Buena Vista. Honorato worked on many of the adobe masonry buildings in Vista, and a brewer back in the mid-1880's. Max also grew up hearing stories about his Uncle Indian Joe, a brewer of beer during 1920's prohibition days. Indian Joe served in WWI and WWII, and today's Vista brewery is named in his honor. Max's background brewing beer dates from days of construction work with his dad. They were employed by an old timer Clutch Kaiser, a German home brewer. He made surprisingly different odd tasting brews much different from the usual Miller's and Michelob they'd open up after work on Fridays. So, the old timer suggested the following Friday they should try beer he'd bottle. From then on, each Friday the old German came back with a new beer brewed in an old 70-gallon dairy tank he had improvised at home. After the fresh brew arrived, the workers had trouble liking it. Max tried tasting German beer and thought, "this is horrible!" But, Max's dad insisted they'd should finish the bottles off, and befriend their employer. Later, Max apprenticed with Clutch Kaiser's brewing equipment in the late 80s, learning the intricacies of brewing a good beer.

Max continued his home brewing routine into 2012, then with his partner Geri Lawson opened a tasting room on La Mirada Drive in Vista. Max brewed several times a day on a 20-gallon system. He was brewing six or seven days a week. "It was getting busier and busier becoming a never ending battle keeping up with the demand," recalled Max, "and our first Vista location never would make enough beer to go out on the market and just enough supplying our 3,500 sq. ft. tasting room. And, we were still growing rapidly."

Vista's popularity also has grown, and rent had doubled after Max's tasting room lease ran out. Gathering resources and deciding taking over a former Trex retail bicycle building on Highway 78, an extended two-year sequence included moving the entire brewery and a very slow process. The 18,000 sq. ft. installation on opening day was still installing Indian Joe's new 15-barrel Premier Brewing system, delivered early 2017. The beer's quality is complimented by uni-tank fermenters/brite tanks creating fresh full beer flavor. Max emphasizes, "there's tremendous number of hours going into brewing usually taking up to 19 hours a day. If things break, I've been a certified electrician but wiring is just one problem, then add on the brew equipment not functioning, or conforming to regulations or anything else." Parties at Indian Joe's brewery in Vista fit up to 300 people and the expanding hours from 11 to 11, 7 days a week is in the plan. A new 1,700 sq. ft. brewery restaurant features wood fired pizza, lasagna, and an outdoor patio with firepits. There are famous barrel-aged sours fermented with wild yeasts. The barrel room is 19,000 sq. ft. storage area, and lies to the far side of the brewery. There's always a noteworthy tour of craft beers highlighting the latest generation of uniquely tasteful beer styles infused with the indigenous traditions of Max's family tree of brewers.

The Indian Joe Brewing Company's 19,000 sq. ft. facility is visible off the Hop Highway 78, in Vista. Exit at Sycamore and turn onto Industrial Court and the highway frontage road.

Sitting at the illuminated Kilowatt Brewing bartop, customers choose from 12 taps of ales and barrel-aged beer featured at their Kearny Mesa Brewery and their Ocean Beach tasting room.

Master brewer Karl Strauss was a significant influence from the start of San Diego's craft renaissance, establishing the first brewpub downtown, in 1989. His image is memorialized at the Sorrento Mesa Brewery Tasting Room and Beer Garden.

Beginning in 2010, Iron Fist's tasting room featured the brewery's specialty award-winning craft selections with food trucks scheduled every Wedsnesday through Sunday.

Iron Fist Brewing Co.

North County Brewery
& Tasting Room
1305 Hot Spring Way #101
Vista, California 92081
Phone: (760) 216-6500

Barrio Logan Tasting Room
1985 National Ave. #1132
San Diego, California 92113
Phone: (619) 255-5818
www.ironfistbrewing.com

Rule Your Taste with An Iron Fist!

Eve, Brandon and wife, Shaina, serve customers at the tasting room in Vista.

The moment you've tried a well-crafted specialty beer fitting perfectly into your day at the Iron Fist Brewing's tasting room, you've definitely discovered one of San Diego's best breweries. The founders, the Sieminski family visited the sacred European beer dynasties during a family vacation and returned home inspiring Brandon, their teenage son to an early career as a craft brewer. All the while, the family enjoyed making wine at home in San Marcos, so the crossover over to home brewing became a new found fascination after discovering European beer styles. The breweries in Vista during 2009-2010 were being rated a resounding

success throughout North County's warehouse communities as Brandon reflects, "at first, it was almost a small fraternity of just a few once upon a time and now from increased business there's a significant economic impact with all the changes. We opened up the brewery just over six and a half years ago. We were one of some 30 breweries at the time, now it's grown to 140. We're a community of brewers because we all love beer and just as passionate about brewing it. At the end of a day, it's really easy to sit down over a beer. Always, with the right beer for the right occasion!"

However, Brandon's brewing skills ended up at a disadvantage at QUAFF, the local brewing club from being slightly under age at the time. Undeterred, his time had been filled looking up on-line courses and the UC Berkeley College syllabus contemplating varied brewing methods and histories. Fully prepared, he had taken notes and talked to friends, then continued brewing as a family ritual. Brandon adheres to the Brewer's Association mandates, "knowing what the brewing process is, what fermentation is, and what's happening during the processes." He follows up with one annoying example, "diacetyl, is a common flaw recognized by most brewers, and one of 500 chemical compounds produced during brewing. It's important knowing why you are getting certain results or any obstacle effecting the beer's outcome." Brandon explains, "the brewing methods are not as much about heating ingredients, but a series of chemical reactions according to the temperature of the grains, water, and following a recipe to the tee providing consistent results. The information is all there, you just have to find it."

The family began crossing over as a professional brewery soon after the realization they were, "brewing more beer to drink for themselves and friends then they ever needed." The most logical path according to Brandon's theory follows climbing a steep learning curve and along the way taking in neighborhood encouragement from AleSmith, Stone, and Lost Abbey. The relationships boosted Brandon's progress as a brewmaster, and he began running the 15-barrel system at Iron Fist Brewing full time, establishing the brewery in 2010. Opening a tasting room the following year, Brandon had turned just 21, and he developed the names and descriptions of his core beer. Brandon's best seller, Renegade Blonde is a crisp, light and mild top-fermented Kölsch style, "and Iron Fist tasting room's best seller hands down more than anything else. Other favorites are, Nelson The ImPALEr, an American Pale Ale with 100% Nelson Hops and a mainstay with a refreshingly light citrus flavor IPA." Just south of San Diego's metro area, Barrio Logan an art community immersed with historical sites is minutes from downtown. It's the San Diego neighborhood of the once popular post-prohibition Aztec Brewery. The town's artistic appeal matches Iron Fist's unique craft beers and sours' craftsmanship at the brewery's second tap and tasting room location. Several specialty Iron Fist beers are bona fide collaboratives with Brandon including with Ken Schmidt, a legendary South Seas brewing expert and feature brewer emeritus of the 2012 Ken Schmidt / Iron Fist / Stone Mint Chocolate Imperial Stout. It was an original created with Brandon at Stone Brewing facilities. The duo brews together at Iron Fist Brewing, adding their incredibly great beer.

Sampling Iron Fist's core beer list includes several farm ales including Hired Hand, a refreshing Saison, and the Spice of Life, a spiced ale exuding bitter orange peel, coriander, brewed with grains of paradise attaining 6.5% abv, and each Belgian style ales. Two more Belgian beers, Dubbel Fisted, a caramel, plum and chocolate blend attains 8.1% abv, and UpRising Trippel IPA finishes with an apple, apricot, plum, citrus tartness. Add on, The Gauntlet Double IPA, a 9.5% abv, and Counter Strike San Diego IPA lightens up at a 6.5% abv adding citrus, mango, pineapple and passionfruit characteristics. The top shelf, Velvet Glove offers a rich Imperial Oatmeal Stout with a velvety dark color and chocolate-coffee overtones. A 9.0 abv, makes a perfect stand alone dessert beer!

JULIAN BEER COMPANY

2307 Main Street
Julian, CA 92036
760-765-3757
www.julianbeercompany.com

Matt Pitman, Co-owner / Head Brewer
Vince Marsaglia, Co-owner
Jeremy Marsaglia, Co-owner, General Manager

When you take the trip along State Route 78's Hop Highway due east, past the backcountry agrarian, riparian rangelands of Ramona and Santa Ysabel, the highway turns abruptly into the town of historic Julian, in the Cuyamaca Mountains. The town folk are excited about their new brewpub, the Julian Beer Company, because it features an over-the-top smokehouse and craft brewery combination. General Manager, Jeremy Marsaglia, and Head Brewer, Matt Pitman, opened the doors of the newly remodeled brewery celebrating the Grand Opening on July 4, 2018. For a time, Matt worked at Bailey's BBQ and Julian Brewing Co., then he recalls, "a new endeavor began when local brewing experts, Vince Marsaglia and his son, Jeremy, and I, became a working partnership. Emerging as a new business, the Julian Beer Company, we spent the next three years remodeling the brewery, expanded the Brewery Barn and rebuilt the brewpub. During brewery's first year, we entered the San Diego International Beer Festival with our American Brown Ale Weasel and brought home a Silver Medal."

Born and raised nearby in Ramona, Matt found himself in the middle of California's craft renaissance, creating what he calls 'Backcountry Beer'. Perfecting his distinctly unique flavors over years, he had established the Julian Home Brewers Association, in 2010. At Julian Beer Co., Matt's brewing recipes have adapted aspects taken from the surrounding countryside, providing an array of craft styles at the brewery. The diversified tap and tasting room features Matt's own Backcountry Beers and treats visitors to a variety of delicious dining, including the brewpub's own wood-fired smoked pork, beef, chicken, and rib

Julian's downtown is a testament to former mining town days of the 1870s. The open deck at the brewery works as a community gathering place for all!

brisquette. As Matt explains, "We smoke our gourmet brisquette in-house and serve great pizzas, inventive salads and entrées with the right companion beer – in a setting of wildlife with turkey and deer roaming the hillsides around you."

The storybook town of Julian is a well known destination for its scrumptious apple pie shops and as a gateway at the 4,226-foot elevation, cresting high above San Diego County. The 1870 Bailey House was the original home of the town's founder, and today houses the brewery's 6-barrel system. The new Julian Beer Company offers a palette of creative tastings and food pairings with up to 21 beers on tap. Matt mentions, "after expanding our equipment we're brewing double batches, adding two 15-bbl fermenters and a 15-bbl brite tank." Matt points out Julian's unique historical origins, "where Coleman Creek runs right under Main Street flowing all the way to Santa Ysabel where hundreds of claims were staked during the 1870s. There are two mines right above the brewery, the Washington and Eagle mines. Over time, the area's nickel and copper mines became the most lucrative."

The most popular beer styles on tap include a juicy ale made with Waimea hops, called The Martian IPA. Another IPA, Trail Angel, features a blend of Golden

Downtown Julian invites all to enjoy its seasonable events.

Promise with Motueka hops. Among Matt's most popular ales, the unique Rye IPA, Pistol Whipped; and an awesome local honey and wheat beer, Silk and Honey; as well, the McCoy Bros. American Ale make lighter session beers. Core lighter ales like Pick Axe Pale Ale, contrasts from a larger tasting, Charlatan, a Belgian Style Strong Ale. And, exploration of darker beers at the brewery offer the smooth pouring Howl Stout, on nitro. Another core and great one, B.A.B. IIPA at 9.8% abv. tops off any search of complex tastings. Others are dry-hopped flavor forward beers, such as, Age or Wisdom? a barrel-aged funky sour ale; or Love Goggle, a lighter apricot mango sour, or others rotated at the brewery. Take home beer crowler and growler fills are available, as well to look for upcoming six-packs; and the maturing wild barrel-aging program.

Visitors may choose from more traditional styles, such as a seasonal Saison beer brewed according to the natural surroundings and seasons. Taking advantage of local sage, rosemary, lavender, apple and pear fruit blossoms, Matt adds a touch of dandelion flowers to a vivacious Hillside Rendezvous Saison Ale. Another traditional beer dates back to over 500 years of sour beers, a Finnish Sahti, and the latest collaborative beer made with Ramona's Smoking Cannon Brewery. It was originally steeped in hollow logs with a matting of Juniper branches atop the grain and exposing the batch to open fermentation of wild yeasts. Back then, the sour beer probably was served as a warm and flat beverage. Today's version offers a tasty modern re-creation. Also, Julian Beer Co. with Julian's Nickel Brewery, collaborated on a Kölsch style beer released honoring the town's 150th Anniversary. It's a creative brew from Matt and Tom Nickel's combined expertise, reflecting a touch of charismatic brewing craftsmanship.

Julian's mountainous geography lies within a confluence of historical trails and missionary paths, developed by California's earliest explorers. The path of the

The historical 1870 Bailey House houses today's brewery. It's founder, Drury Bailey, named the town after his partner, Mike Julian.

Butterfield Stagecoach line from the 1850s traveled far the twists and turns over one-lane roller coaster highways through San Diego County's mountains, deserts and lakes. At the nearby town of Campo, on the United States-Mexico border, the Pacific Crest Trail originates crossing near Julian at Warner Springs, stretching 2,000 miles further to the Canadian border. Many travelers, hikers and campers are drawn to Julian Beer Co.'s hospitality, famous dining and enjoying its premium craft beer. 150 years later, the town has never really conformed to modernity, and you'll see plenty of shops to explore.

Downtown Julian has been a consistent stopover for San Diego residents, who consider the town a local treasure. The Bailey House and brewery became a reality after Matt and his wife, Tawnya, had foreseen opening as early as 2010 with the Julian Beer Company name. Today, the brewery gratefully follows the dream of specially crafted Backcountry Beer for all to enjoy.

A perfect stop for superb meals in the high country, the Julian Beer Co. brewery barn offers a spacious seating and an outdoor deck to enjoy the day.

Kilowatt Brewing renovated a former motorcycle shop into a stunning taproom in Ocean Beach. Kilowatt's tasting rooms display glowing bartops and new age blacklight / LED art.

KILOWATT BREWING

7576 Clairemont Mesa Blvd.
San Diego, CA 92111
858-715-3998

Ocean Beach Tasting Room
1875 Cable Street
San Diego, CA 92107.
619-255-9775
www.kilowatt.beer

Steve Kozyk, CEO / Co-founder
Rachael Fischer, COO / Co-founder
Adam Vance, Co-owner
Nate and Andrea Fischer, Managers

Both Kilowatt Brewing's Ocean Beach and Kearny Mesa tasting rooms are illuminated by an artist's creative spark of imagination for vivid colors matching vibrant beer flavors and full spectrum of craft beer styles. There's always four or five handcrafted IPAs running on 20+ taps, all natural, small batch brewing spotlighting uniquely fresh ingredients. The nano-brewery highlights small batch brewing for experimentation with hop-forward flavor beers. Recently, an entry at the 2019 Great American Beer Festival, in Denver, their OB Bubble Dubbel, a Belgian-Style Dubbel earned a Bronze Medal.

Kilowatt's innovative brewing of single-hop American IPAs into a series entitled Hoptastic Voyage is described by Nate Fischer, "where each beer has everything in the recipe the same including a supporting single malt and single yeast; then each is brewed with a vastly different select single hop." The series Hoptastic Voyage beers include Citra, Kohatu, Dr. Rudi, Galaxy and several rare and unusual hops. Nate points out, "Two of the styles we're known for are barrel and kettle-aged sours defining a distinct wide range of flavors. San Diego's craft beer brings out sophisticated tastes and flavors, and often each beer is determined at the time of brewing when finished. We'll use a Wit beer as a palette for adding flavors like the Coconut-Chai Porter, and a Chocolate Macadamia Nut Stout, and White Chocolate Macadamia Nut Stout are all released simultaneously and popular sellers." The team encourages feedback from patrons and invites collaborations encouraging a platform for a community based brewery and tasting room. A short block away from the Ocean Beach pier, Kilowatt's tasting room and outdoor patio is convenient stopping in for attending the Farmers Market on Wednesdays, or shopping downtown OB. Both of Kilowatt's tasting rooms highlight owner, Steve "Scones" Kozyk's multi-talented illuminated artwork, sculptures, glowing bartops, and stunning black lighting, accenting their brilliant beer tastings produced and bottled in Miramar.

One of Kilowatt's more outrageous pieces of art appropriately sits parked outside, and the brewery's hand painted 1962 Morris Minor, serves as rolling sculptural art and an effective advertisement. Befitting the team's collective air, Kilowatt Brewing's colorful interactive LED lighting, 3-D black light sculpture and phosphorescent paintings pervade the unique tasting room environment for group events, meet ups, and after work happy hours at each one-of-a-kind tap rooms. The brewery suggests guided tastings to take the opportunity to interact and directly enrich your experience at Kilowatt!

Branding carries over with strong support from Kilowatt Brewing Co. supporting stunning artworks, artists and presentation of artful beers.

LATITUDE 33° BREWING

1430 Vantage Court #104
Vista, CA, 92081
760-410-6333
www.latitude33brewing.com

Mike Ingram, President and CEO
Richard Rossi, Associate Brewer

Latitude 33° Brewing's most popular IPAs are synonymous with San Diego's most successfully brewed craft beers. Centered in North County's Vista neighborhood, the brewery's wide ranging audience extends throughout San Diego and the southern California area. Its tasty, best seller introduced in 2015, Blood Orange IPA, initiated a totally new direction to Latitude 33°'s brand, emphasizing the "relentless pursuit to bring the world unparalleled craft." The introduction of Blood Orange IPA was spurred nearly one year after the entrance of Mike Ingram. Initially, Mike's father, Ron, asked Mike to consult as an economic advisor when the brewery had fallen on hard times. However, Mike's relentless spirit proved to be just what the company needed, so he joined the team full-time as President and CEO. From there Mike revamped the business model and led the company to tremendous growth, earning them the title of fourth Fastest Growing Private Company in San Diego by the San Diego Business Journal.

Today, Latitude 33° participates in a multitude of charity events and festivals which has helped build their fan base and help position them at the forefront of craft notoriety known for master brewed approachable flavor styles of fruited west coast IPAs, hazy ales, and rotating porters. Contemplating San Diego's complex craft beer market, Mike Ingram compares past experiences that guide Latitude 33° Brewing towards its goal of brewing tasteful, adventurous flavors.

Latitude 33° has several core offerings including Blood Orange IPA, their flagship brew with a refreshing entry and a crisp, juicy finish. Mangoveza Tropical Mango IPA combines both sweet and heat with a fruity bitterness, followed by a burst of habanero warmth in a well-balanced IPA. Honey Hips Strong Ale features exotic aromas, and a taste of clover honey with a hint of refreshing citrus and spice. Lost Cities Hazy IPA exposes a peak flavor erupting with juicy citrus, and the complimentary Meridian Myst Hazy Pale Ale has a light, tropical seductiveness. Native Trails is a series of rotating Porters that change every couple of months and pursues an unparalleled adventure with flavors like Chocolate Peanut Butter, Blackberry and Blueberry, Vanilla and Coconut.

With year-over-year growth exceeding industry standards, Latitude 33° Brewing is a confirmed San Diego favorite with a dedicated team of 33 employees making it all possible. The brewery's unrestricted approach continues to focus on their home market in San Diego with recent expansion into several key territories, including Orange County, LA and northern California. Collaboration is a large part of the craft industry and Latitude 33° strongly believes it is necessary.

Recently, they teamed up with the neighboring breweries Pizza Port, Burgeon and Culver to craft Bro-kini; a hazy IPA infused with fresh toasted coconut and a hint of vanilla that perfectly encapsulates San Diego summers. As San Diego's outstanding brews arrive in ever increasing numbers, each unique recipe at Latitude 33° captures the imagination by serving finely tuned beers using a high level of craftsmanship.

Like a well-oiled machine, Latitude 33° Brewing's command of consistency and innovation pushes the limits in great beers done well. The Vista tasting room is open daily and offers a world of opportunity to beer enthusiasts echoed in positive affirmation throughout the San Diego community. Latitude 33° beer is available in growlers and found in six packs in recyclable cans, 22oz. bottles and available at over 1000 locations throughout California.

LEGACY BREWING CO.

363 Airport Rd.
Oceanside, CA 92058
760-705-3221
www.legacybrewingco.com

Legacy Tap & Kitchen
7060 Miramar Rd.
San Diego, CA 92121
858-695-9953
www.legacybrewingtapandkitchen.com

Mark Mericle, President/Executive Brewer
John "J.J. "Snyder, CFO/Operations
Andrew Baer, Brewer/Marketing/Events
Britney Kalk, Tap Room Manager

The 40-foot bartop was hand-poured and much of the tasting room is handmade with many recycled features.

Updating their branding in 2017, Legacy Brewing Co. remains a perennial cornerstone landmark just off State Hwy 76 at the Oceanside Airport. Since 2013, the brewery's Mark Mericle, GABF Gold Medal brewer, and John "J.J." Synder, operations manager, had partnered building a team at the brewery under the core principles upholding underlying freedoms we inherited within our American system. Legacy Brewing Co. established the third craft brewery in Oceanside, a small North County coastal town boasting the second longest wooden pier in California. In 1988, Mark Mericle had co-founded Heritage Brewing Co. after an inspirational tour visiting Bavaria, Germany. In a stunning move putting down roots in Dana Point, Mark created and became head brewer at the first craft brewery in Orange County. He has brewed great beer continuously for 35 years. Setting up operations in Oceanside involved hands on skills from the brewery team completing the interior's tasting room and pouring an impressive finely finished bartop stretching 40-feet in length. The brewery's outdoor patio is sunny and balmy. The barroom carries up to 17 taps of Legacy's beers, and the brewery features six or seven core beers on draft any day. Legacy Brewing's homage to our country's early history created a favorite specialty namesake beer for George Washington's favorite, "A Cup O'George honors our country when coffee became the national drink, and people ordered a cup O'George back in the day. Our Cup O'George is an infused Coffee ESB, an extra special bitter ale and a drinkable 5.3% abv. George Washington brewed beer and also owned a large distillery," J.J. points out, "Legacy Brewing's beer is based on American and European traditions, legendary good taste and a great team effort." J.J. also describes how the tasting room's comfortable 1,000 sq ft. was handcrafted and made from recycled wood with earthy overtones. They added a live performance music stage at the brewery's center and music is scheduled every weekend.

Legacy Brewing's sister Tap and Kitchen restaurant presents a top flight tavern just off Miramar Rd., San Diego. Serving fresh Oceanside's draft Legacy beer paired with a tasteful cornucopia of freshly prepared dishes matched to freshly brewed craft beer. Popular choices include spicy Buffalo, Hot, BBQ, and Orange Teriyaki Chicken Wings matched with Hellfire IPA. Hellfire IPA also won the LA International Gold Medal for an ale featuring 8 hop varieties in a balanced beer with a hint of a citrusy mango. Or, sample a delicious Fish and Chips dish with That Guava Beer, a summery fruity ale, soft malt flavor accented with fresh white guavas and tropical aromas. Street style tacos are stuffed with North Atlantic Lobster Rolls topped with homemade Serrano slaw and pickled onions, paired with Legacy's Illuminated Blonde, a refreshing kölsch slightly malty beer features medium bitterness and a dry finish. Legacy Brewing features limited barrel-aged beer editions and beer sours infused in oak, corked & caged in 750 ml bottles. A recent Gold Medal win at 2018's San Diego International Beer Festival was awarded to Legacy's Clan Ross Scotch Ale, a tasty malted ale. The brewery's wall art showcases basic themes of surfing, beer history, and music.

Legacy Brewery's beers are available in cans and bottles of IPA, Guava, Irish Red, Holiday Ale, Scotch Ale, and Lager beers. Cheers!

Little Miss Brewery Miramar brewery tasting room at the far end of Stromesa Ct., Miramar.

LITTLE MISS BREWING

Miramar Brewery & Tasting Room
7949 Stromesa Ct Ste. Y
San Diego, CA 92126
619-880-2752

Normal Heights Tasting Room
3514 Adams Avenue
San Diego, CA 92116

East Village
545 Park Blvd,
San Diego, CA 92101
www.littlemissbrewing.com

Greg Malkin, CEO / Operations Manager
Jade Malkin, Owner / Communications
Mike Morbitzer, Brewmaster
Marci Morbitzer, Tasting Room Manager

At first glance, Little Miss Brewery's warehouse in Miramar appears casually rearranged for taps and tables. The "Beeramar" brewery had been planned for production only in hopes setting up tasting rooms down the road. But all ended up otherwise, and the brewery operating space of 4,000 sq. ft. is filled with brewing equipment and just enough room for visitors to walk around and have a robust beer. The couches and tables are suitable sitting and sampling amazing beer any evening while overlooking a glorious sunset past the loading dock. The second Little Miss Brewing tasting room in Normal Heights near Balboa Park supports the brewery's colorful WWII genre imagery of B-17 bombers, vintage poster art, and paraphernalia identifying the Allied Forces command victories in Europe. The homage to U.S., British and French war memorabilia fits well into the brewery's explosive San Diego debut in 2015. In recent competition at the San Diego International Beer Festival, the brewery won a shiny Gold Medal for their English-Style Brown Ale, Battle Ground Brown. Supercharged with hop forward thinking, team member and former Green Flash brewer, Mike Morbizter has found fun keeping up with the high demands of local accounts. The range of beers parallels the brewery's WWII themes they've chosen matching their American IPAs, New Deal, and Helldiver. Mike is a Certified Cicerone adding, "we have means to identify the strains using three anaerobic bacteria including brettanomyces, pediococcus, and lactobacillus, making beer sours created in varying degrees of flavor. There's three strains of barrel-aged cultures, and one barrel is entirely brett used in making sours. Another blended with brett yields a super-sour beer that's much more tart, or blending all three makes a more balanced combination. The larger wooden barrel in the middle of the brewery is the mother cask used for recharging sours. We keep a series of 'spirit barrels' specifically to make spirit forward barrel-aged beer. Aging sours are ready six months to a year, after the team blends or uses dry hopping. Barrel sours can be poured after four months up to a year and a half, or longer. It depends on what you're looking for."

Over its lifespan, the Little Miss Imperial Stout Devil's Piano, won bronze in the Arizona Strong Beer Competition for the Stout and Porter category. Among other favorites, there's Coffee Patton American Porter, Blitzkrieg Berliner Weisse sour and Red Army IPA. The brewers created the Little Miss S*M*A*S*H Pale Ale Series showcasing varied types of hops notably, Maris Otter, Cascade, Mosaic, Golden Promise, Zythose, Citra with several others. Mike points out, "we've brewed a light Belgian triple blonde right now in barrels ready to transfer, carbonate, and keg. We make an awesome double IPA, 8.5% abv with oatmeal, a classic red IPA balanced between malt and hops. Of a few collaborative beers, one was a hoppy wheat ale shipped to Ballast Point Long Beach where they did the brett program turning out a great sour." On aging the beer, Mike explains along the way it's taste tested and "it's not ready until it's ready." It's a colorful engaging experience at the main brewery in Miramar during brew days. All tasting rooms have colorful vintage decor artwork and surrounded by amazing beers on a daily basis. Enjoy visiting Little Miss Brewing any day after 2pm, and open mid-day on Fridays and weekends.

Longship Brewery

10320 Camino Santa Fe Ste. C
San Diego, CA 92121
858-246-7875
www.longshipbrewery.com

Dan Jachimowicz, Founder / Brewmaster

It's easy imagining how Dan Jachimowicz founded his flagship brewery reflecting from his study of the Viking culture's rich sense of discovery by those early explorers. Today's passion for exploration translates well into Longship Brewery's destiny making great beer. Dan's recipes comprise of a wide assortment of styles serving 14 at a time from the brewery's tap and tasting room. Longship Brewery opened in July 2016, and within a year the tap room was rated #11, "out of the best 50 of America's places to grab a craft beer," according to Yelp's national ratings! If

Dan's metallurgy and design skills on display at the brewery are handcrafted pieces of art.

you're a beer enthusiast, then Longship Brewery offers an adventurous journey over the horizon to select handcrafted ales and lagers.

Located just northeast of Miramar's central cluster of brewery warehouses, Longship Brewery stands alone in a quiet industrial area surrounded by a forested view, as the tasting room's beer remains alone conquering the quest of brilliant aroma and taste. You are greeted at the tap room taking in the unique recreated Viking circular shields lining the walls perimeter, each artfully decorated by friends of the brewery. The European Viking Age began about AD 700 continuing to around 1100, an evolving culture encouraging common work, social gathering, understanding community, and conversation. Newly found

The perfect getaway in Miramar, Longship Brewery features great craft beer, woodland surroundings and handmade artwork. (Courtesy of Longship Brewing)

fortunes and discovery are analogous in the line up of Longship Brewery's original core beers. Current choices include Ragnabock, a dopplebock award-winning dark strong lager leads with a mild ester and roasty sweet aroma. Upon tasting, one is welcomed by dark roasted malt flavor without the bitterness combined with prune-like dark fruit flavors. ShieldWall, an American IPA, and Seafarer, a kettle sour gose widen out the path leading to Olaf the Stumbler, an India Pale Lager, and Valknut-meg, a spiced Brown Ale with nutmeg. The selections include tasteful session choices ranging 4.8 to 6% abv and higher, and Longship's American Strong Ale Abomination peaks at 9.3% abv and 56 ibu, and Althing, a 10.1% 10 ibu Belgian Tripel.

Visitors to the tasting room find a gallery of colorfully hand-painted kaleidoscopic Viking shields and individually designed motifs. They reflect a 1000-year old culture of long ships and voyages transforming an awakening world. The brewery's pledge dedicates making great tasting beer meant to brighten the way. A journey to Longship Brewery Co. carries forward the theme of the brewmaster, "Let the work speak for the craftsmen!"

Helix Brewing Company is tucked into San Diego's industrial neighborhood of La Mesa, the first craft brewery to settle in the East Side. There's a spacious back patio to sit, sip and relax.

San Diego's Kensington Brewing has opened a new brewery tasting room location, re-establishing its roots in the Kensington neighborhood, at 4067 Adams Ave.

Dan Jachimowicz's Longship Brewery Co. in Miramar follows craft brewing in parallel with his craftsman skills of Viking themed art on display at the brewery.

The spacious Common House Urge Gastropub's inside entry to their 15-barrel brewing system.

MASON ALE WORKS

Rancho Bernardo
Urge American GastroPub
16761 Bernardo Center Dr
San Diego, CA 92128
858-673-8743

Urge GastroPub and Common House
255 Redel Rd.
San Marcos, CA 92078
760-798-8822
www.urgegastropub.com

Carmel Valley Mason Ale Works Tasting
Room + Kitchen
5550 Carmel Mountain Rd #113
San Diego, CA 92130
858-261-0603

There's an added touch of grandeur with each succeeding project created by
North County's 3 Local Brothers Restaurant Group in the last decade. Owners,
Grant Tondro, Zak and Nate Higson, were searching for an ideal burger and
beer concept and found after removing the first and last letters of "burger,"
they agreed on "URGE Gastropub", fitting the bill perfectly. Starting out
in 2007, Grant, a certified wine sommelier established Rancho Bernardo's
popular, The Barrel Room Vintage Wine Bar and Bistro. The rising tide of craft
breweries had electrified San Diego's appetite for outstanding brewpubs, and the
brothers decided designing their own reinterpretation of an English pub. The
new restaurant featured 51 taps and as Grant explains, "we started The Urge
American Gastropub in The Plaza in 2010. It was our way of offering craft beer

Mason AleWorks Common House & Gastropub, near the Hop Highway 78, is a 21,000 sq. ft. brewpub, bowling and sports center, bar and restaurant featuring an added 10,000 sq. ft. of outdoor patio space.

on tap from all over San Diego right next to our first establishment. We were completely immersed in the movement of handcrafted foods and beverages in San Diego and opened as a small community restaurant right off I-15 in Rancho Bernardo. Coincidentally, it attracted the attention of many local craft brewery founders as customers, and we became a favorite watering hole for the owners of AleSmith, Stone and Ballast Point over the years. It was something new and different attracting a steady clientele. Our closest competitor had 50 taps, so we became a big deal offering a huge range of great craft beer!"

After 2010, the brothers set out establishing a series of identifiable tasting rooms and brewpubs featuring distinctly comfortable and adventurous settings. The craft beer industry was gathering momentum in San Diego, and the first Urge American Gastropub presentation featured many local craft breweries and became a huge success. Also, the team installed a complex of shops in Rancho Bernardo successfully establishing The Brothers Provisions, a niche American deli with Mason's CoffeeWorks. By 2015, the partnership set their sites on a sleepy Coast Highway corner and remodeling a bank building opened Mason Ale Works and Whiskey Bank with the second Urge Gastropub, in Oceanside. The brewpub restaurant features a full-on 10-barrel brewing system adding to choices of craft beer, spirits, cork, and craft food pairings. The restaurant serves a carefully prepared gourmet cuisine accompanying freshly brewed craft beer

The Mason AleWorks 8-lane bowling alley provides a perfect space accommodating family getaways inside the San Marcos Common House.

or any of Mason Ale's own in-house selections and specialties. In April 2017, the brothers' current concept was unveiled. Dubbed the Mason AleWorks Urge Gastropub and Common House, it's located within a mixed-use shopping and living complex in a 200-acre commercial zone. The new center in a location near the Hop Highway 78 serves as an event venue to the community. The monumental 21,000-square-foot brewpub footprint strategic placement resides within a new mixed-use residential development near Cal State, San Marcos.

At the San Diego International Beer Festival in Del Mar in 2018, Mason Ale's Charley Hustle, American-style Amber/Red Ale won a bright Gold Medal, and a Bronze Medal, the succeeding year. Gunnar Noir, an American-style India Black Ale won a Silver Medal. The brothers outfitted a new 15-barrel brew system and their landmark establishment encompasses all aspects of drinking, dining, and gaming featuring an added 10,000 sq. ft. of outdoor patio space. The Common House has 41 taps serving a capacity of 400 diners at the restaurant. A natural setting for sports enthusiasts, there's an 8-lane bowling alley with a niche bar, big screens, and UV glowing lights illuminating the bowling pins. 101 Proof, an in-house speakeasy serves crafted cocktails featuring 80 whiskey selections. In the outdoor areas, customers enjoy bocce ball, picnics, firepits, Giant Jenga, Cornhole, Connect Four, or idle lounging making this an ultimate getaway destination to see in San Diego.

NEW ENGLISH BREWING

11545 Sorrento Valley Rd. Ste. 305
San Diego, CA 92121
619-857-8023
www.newenglishbrewing.com

Simon Lacey, President / Head Brewer
Nina Lacey, Co-founder/ Marketing

Growing up surrounded by the traditions of British beer and moving to San Diego in 1995, Simon Lacey found a challenge and true proving ground for brewing great craft beer for world class competition. Simon's concept combined the idea of brewing innovative beer from the best "Old World" English styles, adding the fervor of "West Coast" flavors. It's the reason he visualized opening New English Brewing Company in 2007. The results are recognized as New English Brewing's core line up of beer comprises 47 medal winners in 14 different beer styles.

In a highly-esteemed competition, 2016's San Diego International Beer Festival awarded a Gold Medal to Pure & Simple IPA in recognition of complex deliciously well-balanced taste blending four hop varieties (Centennial, Mosaic, Citra, and Amarillo.) There's subtle aromas of guava, mango, and pineapple helping earn 93 points on Rate Beer. It's the brewery's choice ale, if ever marooned on a deserted island at a pleasant 6.5% abv and 75 ibu.

Zumbar Chocolate Coffee Imperial Stout first brewed in 2012, has won six medals in the coffee beer category since its release. It's a core beer style from New English Brewing dominating

several competitions, including winning the 2015 GABF Gold Medal and the 2016 GABF Bronze Medal. Zumbar earned "Best of Show" at the LA County Fair in 2015, and Gold Medals consecutively in 2013, 2014, and 2015. It is a beer that delights the palate with its sultry blend of Belgian dark chocolate and artisan roasted coffee from local roaster Zumbar Coffee and Tea. At 9.3% abv and 45 ibu, this beer is well-balanced with Nugget hops, ensuring a pleasant bitterness offsetting powerful combinations of malt, coffee, and chocolate and earning 99 points on Rate Beer. Winning seven awards, New English Brewing's Brewers Special Brown Ale won the coveted World Beer Cup Bronze Award in 2016. It achieved four Gold Medal wins in consecutive years at the LA County Fair. Brewers Special has a robust and malt character with a hopping rate of 33 ibu, its complex flavor profile is well-balanced, and oh so smooth. At 6.6% abv, beware, as Brewers Special Brown Ale is deceptively easy drinking for its strength!

New English recently opened a 2700 square-foot tasting room, "The Barrel Room" right next door. There's a 32-foot bar and 20 taps, and the Barrel Room houses New English's barrel-aged beers in a upbeat venue often reserved for weddings and private events. Stopping by New English Brewing is an experience to be repeated, and place to imagine the next generation of award-winning beers.

NICKEL BEER COMPANY

1485 Hollow Glen Road & Highway 78
Julian, CA 92036
760-765-BEER
www.nickelbeerco.com

O'Brien's
4646 Convoy St.
San Diego, CA 92111
858-715-1745
www.obrienspub.net

West Coast Smoke & Tap House
6126 Lake Murray Blvd
San Diego, CA
619-462-3660
westcoastbbqandbrew.com

Tom Nickel, Owner / Brewer
Brian Scanlon, Brewer

Tyson Blake, General Manager

Tom Nickel had been drawn to Julian to begin a San Diego brewery, and established the present location, in 2013.

Located in the upper elevations above the fog, Nickel Beer Co.'s tap and tasting room on Hop Highway 78 in Julian, is an important extension of Tom Nickel's focus in respect to San Diego's craft beer business. As a native of San Diego discovering home brewing at age 18, he was too young to buy beer and learned you could do-it-yourself from a friend, and continued devoting a singular passion towards enjoying the brewing business in many creative ways. Julian's Nickel Beer Co. building is a true piece of Americana, and once former Sheriff Department's outpost and holding department, stands firmly today as a full-fledged craft brewery. The head brewer, Brian Scanlon keeps the 16 taps flowing at the tasting bar, while brewing enough for the company's two satellite pubs near San Diego's downtown.

Nickel Beer Co.'s rustic western tap and tasting room bar, just outside Julian's downtown.

You'll find core beers include an exceptionally light and pleasantly hopped, Take A Hike Extra Pale Ale; as well as the award-winning Warrior Golden Ale, a signature beer aiding military women at the nearby non-profit Inner Northstar PTSD Retreat Center, located in Julian. Another collaboration commemorates Julian's 150th Anniversary recently premiering at the brewery and throughout town. Nickel's Stonewall Stout pours as black as night, packing a massive flavor punch, blended with roasted and crystal malts, with hints of coffee flavors. Two favorites, Volcan IPA, and C.C. O'Neill's Irish Red Ale, each are classic West Coast brews. A popular hybrid, Apple Pie Ale, or 'pie in a glass' is made with local winesap apples, blended in a beer base and spiced with cinnamon, ginger, nutmeg, allspice and clove. Each beer is enhanced by the rustic landscape and mountain air, as locals and visitors enjoy savoring beer and bringing take home growlers for fills at the Nickel Beer Co.'s unique scenic tasting room location.

Tom's affinity with professional brewing began in 1994, soon after his return from college back East. He was a quick learner awestruck by San Diego's rise of local craft breweries, "and decided before I spend my life in a suit and tie, in finance or some terrible thing like grad school, I literally called every brewery in California and asked if there was a job, and got two days a week in summer filling in at the Linda Vista Home Brew Mart. Then, one of the main employees moved out, married his girlfriend in Missouri, and I stayed on managing the

mart for 2 1/2 years, as they established Ballast Point. We didn't have the idea of a tasting room and back then handed out 4oz. samples. I was the original tasting room employee and there were only four taps and a tasting bar." Soon after, Tom went off to Pizza Port, "where I worked with Tomme Arthur and founded a couple of festivals including developing Pizza Port's Strong Ale Festival, now in its 23rd year." Beginning 1998 and through 2005, he was head brewer at Stuft Pizza in Delmar, and ended up at their chain's production facility in San Clemente for well over a year. In a team with Jeff Bagby in 2004, they won the World Beer Cup Small Brewery of the Year at GABF. Soon, the brewpubs rebranded to become Oggi's Brewery.

"On January 1, 2003, an opportunity came up to acquire an American style pub, O'Brien's in Kearny Mesa, and although still brewing I had two jobs." O'Brien's pub is headed today by General Manager and Beer Curator, Tyson Blake; and later, Tom Nickel opened the West Coast Smoke & Tap House in La Mesa. The tavern has been rated in the top 100 Beer Bars in the USA. Each pub features 28 taps of premium craft beers and represents a wide variety of statewide beer choices, as well as Nickel Beer Co.'s own rotating 15 beers.

In 2007, as a pro brewer, Tom helped found the San Diego International Beer Festival, now the largest beer festival on the West Coast with its well known highly regarded top honors' competitions based on blind judging, with as many as 1,564 entries from 291 different breweries, spanning 23 U.S. states and 20 countries. Held annually at the Del Mar Fairgrounds, each entrant at

At Nickel Beer Co. in Julian, the old sheriff's office has been repurposed into an 'Old West' style bar and brewery with 16 taps.

the festival seeks the most coveted of all awards: Best of Show, and Champion Brewery, hotly pursued among brewery personnel. Both Nickel and Tyson are the 'Beer Coordinators' for the annual festival held in late June. Other events include a range of beer paraphernalia and gifts, wearables, and even something for your family dog! There are ongoing educational presentations presented on food pairing, brewing, beer judging, and general suds sciences. A ticket to the San Diego International Beer Festival includes a day at the fairgrounds and the largest county fair in the entire United States, and there is a Beer Garden featuring many choices of food fare and array of craft beer specialties.

"We have local producers of ingredients nearby, and each year I do a lot with wet hops. Featuring freshly harvested local hops, Hook in Mouth Chinook Wet Hop IPA uses malt from Imperial Valley, yeast from San Diego's White Labs, and hops from Star B Ranch in Santa Ysabel, the largest hop grower in the county. Just adding Julian's well water, there's a completely local produced beer from the area, served at our tasting room." Tom explains further that Julian's well typically has harder water, making it ideal for robust IPAs and Stout beers. What's evident about Tom Nickel's impressive resume is an extensive experience regarding San Diego's beer that certainly qualifies him as an authentic craft beer ambassador in 'America's Capital of Craft'.

Novo Brazil Brewing Co.

901 Lane Ave.
Chula Vista, CA 91914
619-869-4274
www.novobrazilbrewing.com

Eduardo Petagna, Owner/ Master Brewer

(Courtesy of Novo Brazil Brewing Co.)

Chula Vista's inviting southern exposure brings visitors to a new destination brewery tap and tasting room at Novo Brazil Brewing Co. The colorful entryway leads through the brewery's giant open space overshadowed by the large 25-barrel brew system and 19 tall fermenters standing in the background. Novo Brazil Brewing Company's visually impressive brewery brings instant awareness of cultural sounds, colors, and unique beverages meant for peak enjoyment. The town of Chula Vista lies just seven miles from the border and is San Diego County's second largest neighborhood. Novo Brazil Brewing celebrates their award-winning beer brewed by Eduardo Petagna. "We're relatively young but one of the larger breweries in San Diego. We serve at least 15 beers on tap any day, as well as distribute kegs, bottles and cans. Our goal brings culture to the beer traditional styles like Belgium triples or quads and adding a twist for something unexpected." Mulata, is a well-balanced Amber Ale style with specialty malt characteristics and recent Bronze Medal winner at the San Diego International Beer Festival. One of biggest and best sellers, The Mango, offers a hint of mango but at the end of the day you have an IPA. The masterworks of Novo Brazil continues earning prestigious awards after the brewery's opening in 2015. Cookie Muncher, an American Strong Ale is Barrel Aged at 12% abv,

Novo Brazil's entryway into the brewery is highlighted by a Brazilian flair for vibrant colors.

and the World Beer Awards for the Best Dark Strong beer in 2016 and 2017. Also, Chula Pils was best in the US for a Czech-style pale lager in 2016 and 2017. World Beer Awards honored a Gold Medal in 2016 for the Imperial dark beer Belgian style strong Quadrupel, and a Silver Medal in 2017 for Barrel-Aged Quadrupel.

At the San Diego International Beer Festival in 2018, Novo Brazil's Belgian Dark Ale, Quadruppel, and American Style Pale Ale, Rio, each won Silver Medals. Winning Bronze in 2017, at the World Beer Awards, Novo Brazil's British-styled Imperial Stout, Corvo Negro was chosen out of 53 entries. The Country Award was received for the United States at the 2016 World Beer Cup and considered higher than gold in the world of competitive brewing. Consecutive Gold Medals were awarded in 2016 and 2017 for Nova Brazil's Otay IPA as the World Beer Awards' Best IPA in the U.S. On special occasions the brewery brings Samba dancers, Brazilian and Reggae music performances. All this after being open for just two years, and Nova Brazil Brewing's Second Anniversary was celebrated on April 8, 2017, making it Chula Vista's cornerstone destination for brewery visitors and residents alike.

OCEAN BEACH BREWERY

5041 Newport Ave.
Ocean Beach, CA 92107
619-955-8053
www.obbrewingco.com

Scott Watkins, General Manager
Jim Millea, Brewmaster

When it's time to kick back from a day at the beach, a first choice for healthy sea air and a brewpub, is the town of Ocean Beach. When it comes to a spectacular view and first choice craft beer, OB Brewing recently was chosen from a list of 177 entries for its pale ale, winning the 2018 Gold Medal at the GABF, in Denver.

GM, Scott Watkins explains, "our Golden Pale Ale, B.Right On, has a subtle bitterness that's not too dry. It's mostly brewed with Cascade that is dry hopped, and around 40 - 45 ibu. It was dedicated to 'Brighton Street' in OB, the place where Jim Millea, our brewer lived. That year, we won three top honors with the GABF gold medal. One award went to Jim, as the Best Small Brewpub Brewer, and another for the Best Small Brewpub in the nation! Brewing fresh craft, our customers choose from seven to eight rotated OB beers on tap, and we offer selections of other awesome drafts, as well."

Take in an elevated view perched at the top of OB Brewery's incredible rooftop brewpub patio.

OB Brewery's brewpub building, standing 3-stories tall on Newport Ave. rises above the fray, via stairs or elevator and features an incredible 360° view from the rooftop, overlooking the Pacific shoreline. At left center view, the 1966 concrete pier measures as the longest one in southern California. Known for shopping, sightseeing and dining, Ocean Beach is a classic San Diego beach town, and Scott emphasizes, "there's only one thing to do when coming to Ocean Beach…It's about *Slowin' it down! It flows, and it's gonna happen!* …so, if you're from out of town, or even when I come to OB, everything slows down."

Jim Millea brews a pantheon of award-winning traditional styles including the brewery's German style malt-forward, Hidden Gem Dunkleweisen, a dark wheat style ale and Silver Medal winner in 2017, at GABF. Also, Roof Top Saison, won a Bronze Medal at the San Diego International Beer Festival in 2018, and another Bronze Medal for their malt forward, hop forward, Elevator Red IPA. "We have a range of IPAs including a citrus forward Mosaic focused IPA, and a hazy IPA; so in San Diego as anyone might know, our water is made for dank IPAs because it's naturally bitter. We do filter the water and adjust each beer according to a recipe depending on which style we're making. For instance, water itself lends East Coast IPA own styles, when back there the beer is softer, more juicy and fruity. Whereas, West Coast styles are naturally citrus, dank and more bitter."

The brewery has an equal demand for stouts and porter beers, so they brew, Don't Deporter Mé, a robust porter; and their Night Moves on nitro, a rich oatmeal stout reminiscent of a Guinness Cream Stout, with added coffee and chocolate notes. Literally, the brewery's hottest beer is Couples Therapy, a Jalapeño Saison that ranks as light, downright tasty brew creeping up on the backend with a serious green peppery flavor. "The secret behind this recipe," Scott remarks, "this type of beer is often a Pilsner or lighter beer base, but we decided to use our Rooftop Saison because you'll get some sweetness. Adding the pepper, you need a dry light beer to balance the flavor out. As your keep drinking it, the balance between the throat and the mouth becomes more prominent towards the front, eventually taking over the entire palette. You'll find the saison is very light with notes of coriander, white pepper, and a slight sweetness with a dry finish from the yeast, and great for its full flavor and lightness when it's hot out. With the Jalapeño beer, Jim pours off a pony keg of saison in order to steep the peppers directly for two days, just like brewing tea. He starts out with seven pounds of peppers, and six pounds are bruised and blended, and one pound roasted. Then, everything is blended together, adding just the right amount of sweetness. We taste test it and allow it to steep in the brite tank, again it's tasted adding more jalapeño flavor to balance it out when necessary."

Visitors to Ocean Beach will find two square blocks, around Cable and Newport

Ave., with several recognizable San Diego craft brewery names. Scott describes the town's communal ethos emphasizing resistance to fundamental changes and staying true to its nature by keeping an awareness about it's being a living historical seaside landmark. Downstairs, a small tap and tasting room bar provides a streetside niche with tables, and there's a game room hangout on the second floor. At the rooftop level, there's spacious dining and small bar with comfortable table settings and an amazing view. The kitchen is tucked away with a 5-barrel brew system, three 10-barrel fermenters and a 10-barrel brite tank.

Scott recounts, "after a three-year build out, the brewpub opened July 1, 2016. We tend to move numbers of kegs locally, making it hard keeping our beer in stock, and so we are expanding our equipment with our agenda. Everything is made from scratch, and we have top quality bar food and really good salads, vegan options, great wings and burgers, fish and chips, and all our sauces, hummus, guac, are all made in house. Other dishes include carnitas nachos, fish tacos, shrimp tacos, beer wings, and wraps, and our 'B L A S T', a BLT with avocado and salmon, each are fresh and top quality choices." Ocean Beach still maintains the identity of a 1960s-1970s beach town, and as a destination brewpub, the Ocean Beach Brewery aptly fits the description of a cozy beach town bar and brewpub, serving great beer.

Cable Street at Newport, at the center of OB's stretch of downtown shops. There are over half a dozen craft breweries within walking distance from the Ocean Beach Brewery on Newport Ave.

OCEANSIDE BREWING COMPANY

312-314 Via Del Norte
Oceanside, CA 92058
(760) 453-7900
www.oceansidebrewingco.com

Greg Distefano, Owner / Master Brewer
Tomas Bryant, Owner / Brewer

It's no huge surprise the Oceanside Brewing Company pops up as national favorite, recently rated #6 on Yelp's on-line list of bests. The brewery is located just a few miles east of the pier and harbor, near Mission Blvd. Oceanside Brewing Company provides moments of unique tasting experience gained from decades of brewing and celebrating an innovative master's touch using only real ingredients. Greg Distefano, and Tomas Bryant have combined years of knowhow producing well-balanced beer riding high on the wave popular breweries in San Diego County.

It's a destination brewery featuring the most meticulously brewed pure traditional styles adding a touch of West Coast in each glass.

The brewery's location at 314 Via del Norte is situated in a spacious warehouse and features an airy outdoor patio. The climate is perfect for tasting craft beer and enjoying the lightness of a sea breeze. Opening the doors in 2016, Greg's and Tomas's recipes dedicate seasonal, as well as trend setting themes into their craft. Reflecting on what they like to brew comes directly from their coastal lifestyle and past unified friendship as co-partners, sharing time in the

Oceanside Brewing Company's team, Tomas and Greg have been partners over decades. They are award-winning brewers using top quality ingredients. The tasting and tap room is open everyday, on a quiet corner and just east of the Oceanside Pier. ...Cheers!

art of wave riding, yoga meditation, and today's boutique brew house. "The brewery's close to everything, but not in everything," as Greg likes to describe, "it's solitary and away from the more crowded streets."

Keeping up with the brewery's Facebook site, craft beer seekers continue to exclaim joyful reactions over frequent brewery events and newly released beer centered on the duo's single essential purpose of taste and flavor goals and never extracts, ever. OBC's image echoes loudly within San Diego's brewing community traditions of brewing the most choice ingredients into creative beer styles. There's always an added measure of quality, consistency, and guaranteed freshness adding diverse choices including Pours Light, an Helles lager, Strawberry Fields For Now, Jimmy Hoppa and Summer Picnic Watermelon Beer. On any single day the brewery offers selections and varieties of beer poured from 22 taps. Using traditionally sourced malt and hops, they have an edge just a few doors down working with North County's premier yeast maker, Dr. James Pfau, a PhD scientist at Real Brewers Yeast. Yeast imparts magic flavors adding to each recipe's aroma and taste. The differences of yeast will drastically affect tasting for any beer judge, aficionado, or novice. The brewery continues expanding their selections using fresh whole fruits and absolutely no processed ingredients. Setting up Oceanside Brewing started back in the day when San Diego's breweries could be counted on two hands. The initial intent of opening the brewery began 15 years before in 2001 but waiting for new regulations slowed down the process. Greg had already secured the moniker, "Oceanside Brewing Company". Starting out a company after a 27-year brewing background meant he had accrued many hundreds of winning citations and medals as a home brewer. He always aimed balancing craft beer with distinctly complex brewing recipes. During his years brewing for many San Diego professionals, he was already contributing to the rising craft scene. After Greg became head brewer at Stuft Pizza, the chain branched out into Oggi's Pizza and Brewery, and he decided timing was right to join with the few craft labels in Oceanside. However, to obtain a brew house operation permit in Oceanside business council was unfamiliar with breweries, and at that time unable foreseeing the craft beer gold rush of today.

Opening in 2013, there was an handcrafted and impressive tasting room with an ideal breezy beer garden patio added to Oceanside's destination brewery scene. Oceanside Brewing's improved visibility came together with partner, Tomas Bryant, and consists of a team serving a wide choice of freshly brewed specialties. During St. Patrick's Day, a special-released beer included a rich malty Irish Stout named We All Fall Down. A taster's favorite, Porter's Paradise is a smooth brown beer combining hand-toasted coconut flakes, chocolaty flavors using the house porter. Each draft beer is equally balanced unlike any other brewery tap! Common Sense a California Common beer is otherwise known as steam beer, historically going back brewing cold fermenting lagers in the western frontier. Back then refrigeration was not readily available and colder surviving yeasts were allowed to ferment at warmer temperatures. The result was a beer developing some crispness yet displaying more fruity qualities from a less constrained fermentation process. This beer is generally an amber to brown color. Now that you know.... it's time to try it out! Greg's craftsmanship carries over also being a long time master plumber in the region and has installed brewing systems and makes repairs when needed at several local breweries. Greg also founded San Diego Brew Techs and continues centering on, "successfully bringing the craft brewing atmosphere to the local and greater community. Our goal combines history and the creation of the many different styles of ales and lagers continually celebrating Oceanside's uniqueness and traditional values."

A jewel on the North County coast, Oceanside Brewing Co. is a destination craft brewery run by long time resident brewers featuring a full compliment of top ingredients and freshest brews.

Will Fox and his uncle, Ku'uipo welcome visitors to PIB's relaxing Aloha theme tasting room and patio in Santee. Enjoy the heartfelt crafted beers in a true Ohana expression of friendship!

The Novo Brazil Brewery's tasting room setting is intimate, also in full view of the brewing operations. The bar is open Sunday through Wednesday, in Chula Vista.

Today's CAVU Restaurant and Brewery has revived and rebranded La Jolla Brewing Co., in 2018. It's open for lunches and dinners seven days, at 7536 Fay Ave, in La Jolla.

PACIFIC ISLANDER BEER CO.

8665 Argent St. Suite B
Santee, CA 92071
619-270-7777
www.pibbeer.com

Ku'uipoaloha Lawler, Co-Founder
Will Fox, Head Brewer & Co-Founder

Mahalo from the brewers of PIB beers! An island style outdoor patio leads to a south sea theme paradise inside the tasting room and a true Ohana (family) feeling...

The Pacific Islander Beer Company speaks to the passion of brewing craft beer and inviting visitors to an island oasis, just off State Highway 52 in Santee. The brewery's goal maintains the same principles from its beginning, using only the right combination of hops, malts, and natural flavors with an Aloha spirit shared freely to all. Head Brewer, Will Fox's uncle and co-founder, Ku'uipoaloha Lawler seeks to serve each beer like a crashing wave of fine flavors reminding one of a special moment finding themselves in the Pacific Islands. Head Brewer, Will Fox relates, "I was born in Santee and raised in San Diego, graduating from Santana High School in 1994. Back in 2008, I decided I wanted to start home brewing and met Lars Gilman, a true brewmaster and owner of Breakwater Brewing, as well as the Hydrobrew Home Brewing Supply, in Oceanside. He taught me to home brew, and I ran with it. In 2013, Ku'uipo and I began planning Pacific Islander Beer Co., and after a year searching for a building and securing investors, we opened PIB in June of 2015. "Again, I turned to Lars and asked if he could train me on his commercial equipment. He took me under his wing to get going on my path to being a professional brewer."

Ku'uipo and Will's brewery required combining ideas and making all the no's turn into yes's. Ku'uipo remembers, "a long time friend and co-founder, Bob Strangman had listened to my demands while pushing the cart up the hill. Knowing how hard work would lead to living my dream, I found experience is great on paper but it's just paper. What counts is what I am willing to learn every day from hard work. Customers are a great help for a growing business. Just ask them for help and you will grow."

Driving to the town of Santee take the Hwy 52 exit to find PIB Pacific Island brewery at the corner of Argent and Prospect, and the first complex of industrial buildings facing the street. Will and Ku'uipo extend to all, "much Aloha to all our customers that take a moment out of their lives and share drinking our islander spirit filled beer!"

PARIAH BREWING COMPANY

3052 El Cajon Blvd, Suite B
San Diego, CA 92104
619-642-0545

Brian Mitchell, CEO, Brewmaster
Steven Sabers, Co-Founder / Brewer

There are few exceptions for spending an afternoon or evening and tasting better beer than sampling craft at Pariah Brewing Co. In San Diego's North Park, Brian Mitchell is owner and brewmaster taking the art of traditional brewing skills one step beyond. The brewery's 10-bbl brewing system meets the brewery's needs to produce great beer with professional integrity. "We're really trying to brew unlike any other in the county. Besides the option having great beer all around, we want to stand out as unique making the product better. Everything is sourced organically when possible, always real and natural. We try to make ingredients the star of the recipe."

Brian and Steven Sabers, co-owners have thought about beer in a culinary sense, how beer relates to foods, and "how beer is just a fermented soup of grains, and the spices are hops." Of course, there's yeast fermenting it. Regarding the yeast Brian explains, "I have several proprietary types banked at White Labs nearby. This includes one strain picked out years and years ago, a house ale

		QUARTER	FULL POUR
OFF WHITE WIT	BELGIAN-STYLE WITBIER BREWED W/ ORANGE BLOSSOM HONEY, JASMINE GREEN TEA, LEMONGRASS, ORANGE SLICES AND GINGER 5.4% ABV	15 IBU	$2.50	$6.00
DORCHA EXTRA STOUT	FOREIGN EXTRA STOUT BREWED W/ LOCALLY ROASTED COFFEE, COCOA NIBS AND MOLASSES 7.2% ABV	31 IBU	$2.50	$6.00
EROTIC CITY	ALE BREWED W/ ORANGE BLOSSOM HONEY, MUSCAT GRAPES AND GRAINS OF PARADISE 9.0% ABV	20 IBU	$2.50	$6.00
DANK DRANK IPA	HOP-BURSTED WEST COAST INDIA PALE ALE 6.6% ABV	66 IBU	$2.50	$7.00
DRUPE FRUIT IPA	WEST COAST INDIA PALE ALE BREWED W/ PEACH FLESH, MANGO FLESH AND HEMP OIL 7.5% ABV	75 IBU	$2.50	$7.00
UNI STOUT	WINTER SEASONAL STOUT BREWED W/ SAN DIEGO SEA URCHIN ROE, LACTOSE SUGAR AND SEA SALT 5.4% ABV	20 IBU	$2.50	$6.00
MAYOR AND THE MONK	HOP FORWARD ABBEY INSPIRED ALE THAT DRINKS LIKE A SAISON THAT HAS BEEN HOPPED LIKE A CZECH PILSNER 6.0% ABV	36 IBU	$2.50	$6.00
DORCHA ON NITRO	FOREIGN EXTRA STOUT BREWED W/ LOCALLY ROASTED COFFEE, COCOA NIBS AND MOLASSES ON NITRO 7.2% ABV	31 IBU	$2.50	$6.00
CLEARLY JUICE DIPA	JUICE-MASTER DOUBLE IPA WITH MOSAIC, SIMCOE, COLUMBUS HOPS AND MOSAIC LUPULIN POWDER 8.0% ABV	77 IBU	$2.50	$7.00

#PARIAHBREWINGCO #DRINKLOCAL #BETHECHANGE #EROTICCITY

@PARIAHBREWINGCO (STALK/LOVE/SPREAD/REPEAT)

| COLD BREW COFFEE | MODERN TIMES COLD BREWED COFFEE SERVED ON NITRO! ALSO AVAILABLE IN RECYCLED ENVIRONMENTALLY FRIENDLY TOGO CUPS NON-ALCOHOLIC | $6.00 |

yeast referred here as our Wicked Ale Yeast, an English variety that aggressively ferments a batch of ale in three days. It is pretty much used in all our cleaner tasting American-styled ales. Then, I had picked up another proprietary strain in Belgium on our honeymoon. So far, it's been used for our Spring seasonal saison. White Labs collects our yeast, stores them and determines when they are pure."

One yeast harvest recently occurred when Brian and a friend were home brewing wild ales using yeast they found in the garden's bougainvillea flowers. They dropped a flower in some mash allowing it to release ambient spores. Low and behold, a new strain began fermenting the brew. It turned out there were three wild strains, after White Labs determined they had two brettanomyces and a third lactobacillus strain on the flower. "So we have a native North Park beer made from our own variety." Sours with wild yeast are kept in wooden barrels at the brewery, and soon there will be a beer introduced as a bottle conditioned beer originating from North Park.

There's a feeling you've discovered the baddest beer in town, and your experience will prove you right. Pariah's tasting room manager offers a gregarious welcome and begins the discourse exploring Pariah's beer. "We are fanatical – and quite probably even zealots – when it comes to doing it our own way. Our way means we never, ever settle." Choices begin with Off White, a Belgian style Witbier brewed from a complex recipe, and includes Orange Blossom honey, Jasmine green tea, Lemongrass, Orange slices and Ginger, making a refreshingly delicate beer. The Dank Drank IPA is true West Coast style and lives up to Brian's proprietary "hop bursting" technique for India Pale Ale exuding aromas of mango, citrus, peach, pine, berries with ridiculous flavors and aromas, while keeping the bitterness in check! A winter seasonal beer described by Brian, "Our Uni-Stout was made from sea urchin roe harvested off Catalina Island and considered to be the most choice. It seemed like a no-brainer since Japan imports the best roe from California. So why not create something entirely different? It's both an exotic and hyper-locally brewed beer. My wife suggested it because she wanted something along the lines of oyster stouts we both enjoy, so I created a beer to make the best version possible. There's hints of chocolate malt, roasted barley, pilsner malt and minimum of hops fermented with proprietary yeast, milk sugar to balance out the added sea salt and delicacy of the sea urchin roe."

It should not be too hard detecting, there's an abundance of ambition behind brewer Brian Mitchell's creating something great. He's probably as close as you can get to craft beer's Prodigal Son, a devotee expressing a deeper intent. His obsession brewing beer precisely and uniquely has been the founding principle of the brewery in San Diego's North Park. Pariah Brewing Company had become part of the H.G. Fenton "Beer Igniter", a program designing and outfitting micro-breweries, founded in 2016. There's a significant hi-tech advantage at Brian's brewery using a formidable looking 10-barrel brewing and series of 20-barrel fermenters. Pariah Brewing's uncompromising attitude makes for lots of work and plans producing up to 2,000 barrels annually. Water, a key element, is reformulated at the brewery adding balance to the beer's taste. Brian strips away everything using RO, computerized reverse osmosis tailoring an exact profile for each recipe. Beer has become the new rhythm of Brian's once enterprising musical career. It's been a singular path as a professional craft discovering the beauty in making harmoniously satisfying beer. "If you're looking for something unique, progressive, challenging - but ultimately very rewarding - then our beer is for you, our fellow pariahs."

Pacfic Beach Alehouse, at 721 Grand Avenue has stood over years as a neighborhood brewpub. Choose from a range of beers, enjoying rooftop dining within walking distance to the ocean.

Prohibition Brewery patio space has spacious table settings for families, lunches and dinners with a choice of high quality craft beers.

PROHIBITION BREWERY COMPANY

2004 E. Vista Way
Vista, CA 92084
760-295-3525
www.prohibitionbrewingcompany.com

Fallbrook Station
136 N. Main Ave.
Fallbrook, CA 92028
760-645-3443

Visit Google Earth's 360° virtual tour online and see inside Prohibition Brewery.

Prohibition Brewing Co. provides spacious grounds at the brewery for casual dining and beer tasting just four miles from Vista's downtown on East Vista Way. The stand alone "speakeasy" roadhouse double doors open to a carefully crafted oasis in a laid back atmosphere. It's become the perfect place for sampling the local brewpub's freshly craft beer with delicious food pairings. Although modern to the core and designed by its owners, Kathy and Ron Adams, Prohibition Brewery's ambiance of wooden hues and subtle lighting set off vintage memorabilia reflecting the freedoms enjoyed before Prohibition's ominous 18th Amendment became law.

Following 11-11-2011, Prohibition Brewery's Grand Opening, the brewery received top honors. Most recently at 2018's San Diego's International Beer Festival, a Gold Medal was awarded to Prohibition's British Style Strong Ale, Ruby Red. The success followed the previous year's Gold Medal American-style Strong, Hop Chronicles Pale Ale, honoring its golden color reflected by

blended Mosaic and Belma hops showcasing a crisp dry flavor, exuding a slight guava aroma. The Irish-style Red Ale earned Prohibition Brewing a Gold Medal for a medium malt body, deep caramel red ale and roasted barley flavor's smooth finish. Topping off the season during 2016, the Prohibition team won the "Small Business of the Year" for the 36th CA Senate District. Reflecting over the last six years, Ron points out "the brewpub's concept proves to be working well after counting the locals and visitors arriving daily. Currently, there's around 140 breweries in San Diego actively brewing and open to the public. Some are more refined, and the biggest breweries have more automation using computerized conveyors measuring exact amounts. The goals seem some of the biggest breweries get the beer in, done, and out. For us it's meant to be fresh as first made when opened. Craft beer may sustain the flavors for only a month or two and after that begins to degrade."

If you prefer a tempting full menu with food and beer, the brewery uses fresh local ingredients matching its myriad flavors on tap. The menu commands the respect of Prohibition restaurant's true "bona fides" offering the Godfather, a turkey and pastrami sandwich, along side the Lucky Luciano, layered prosciutto and capicola, melted provolone cheese sandwich. Both deserve their namesake's legendary acclaim. Highly rated by locals and visitors alike, Ron's steaks, ribs, fried food, and fresh beers have made this a local destination family getaway. The brewery's flagship beer, ProCo IPA, won a Silver Medal as the American-Style India Pale Ale at the 2019 San Diego International Beer Festival, a hop forward fruity flavor IPA with subtle floral aromas, and the smoother Tin Lizzie features hints of irresistible chocolate and coffee aromas. Ron's favorite recommendation has been the clam chowder coupled with a seared ahi salad, dressed with mango picante. His meals are light enough to sample blond-style ales like his Chech My Pils lager, or a hoppier ale called Derringer IIPA, and even a fresh sensational Vanilla Cream Ale.

It's a tasteful setting commemorating the colorful days of the 1920s, and the theme before, during, and after prohibition's 13 long years. The persistently unpopular law had thrown tap rooms, taverns and saloons into total disarray affecting the industries of entertainment, breweries, distilleries, and restaurants, ultimately dividing a nation. The ban on alcoholic beverages was ratified on January 16, 1919, and all brewing businesses closed by law mid-January, 1920. Few beer industries reemerged at the time of the repeal on December 5, 1933. Memorabilia from the era reflected in Prohibition Brewing Company's polished glossy wood furniture, long bar, large tables, and even spacious patio adds comfortable handcrafted seating. There's commemorative tommy gun wall lamps, a photo gallery of mobsters, and a turn of the century upright piano. It's a step back to a bygone era and perfect location for a friends and family to gather.

After trial brews were started in 2004 inside his home shop, Ron always had earned a consistent praise. "We wanted to start modifying our old system into a slightly different configuration. We worked out our recipes of home brewing into professional brewing and ended up making great beer by doing diligence reading how to formulate recipes with balance." Jay Dominy, head brewer follows Ron's brewing recipes and has full reign over beer production. At the center of brewing operations Jay relates, "our supplies are shipped from grains grown in Yakama Valley, Washington, and Oregon, as well as northern California. Fresh harvests provide natural grains for malts like barley and wheat, although specialty hops and malts might be imported from places like Europe, Australia, and New Zealand."

The brewery expanded with a new brewing system installation across from the patio. Brewing had been tucked away for six years in a niche inside the restaurant's dining room. With the increasing demands of more capacity prompted moving to the new facility. The brewery system will more than double capacity from the original 10-barrel system. The master brewer, Jay arrived at Prohibition Brewery after home brewing became his passion, earning a California UC San Diego post-graduate brewing degree and joining Ron in California in October, 2016. He began using a small brew system making 310 gallons, or approximately 20, 15-gallon kegs every week. The installation allows Jay to use new 20-barrel fermenters and quadruple output. Jay sees Prohibition's productive climb as part of what's been happening throughout North County, San Diego. "It's important to realize San Diego's brew culture began its algorithmic climb right after 2011 from 40 established breweries to maybe 50. Then from 2015-16 another doubling occurred."

The Prohibition Brewing team has brought wide attention as a favorite destination in North County, with a spacious meeting place and patio for groups up to two hundred.

Ron's original career as an electrical contractor was suddenly preempted when his wife Kathy made the decision working together on transitioning into becoming a professional brewery. After a career at Vista High Schools, Kathy began working with Ron on designing and setting up the operation. Opening on September 11, 2011, Prohibition Brewery taps poured fresh ales with dozens of dark stouts, lighter ales, and IPAs, breaking out the many home brew recipes developed over the years. "Starting a pro brewery after home brewing and moving up is not as simple as using bigger equipment," Ron emphasizes, "it's not as if you can make one keg and think it's nothing increasing to five kegs. Only trial and error trying multiples of yeasts, hops, grains, and charting the recipe on paper gains any success."

An important ingredient is yeast, and there are wild yeasts everywhere," Ron explains. "You want a groomed, maintained, and well pampered brewers' yeast, and wild yeasts may be more aggressive and destroy the process. The result of depriving oxygen allows the yeast to eventually become dormant, so we control yeast flow. Timing and temperature are critical because if either changes each variation ends up tasting differently."

All of Prohibition Brewing Company's ingredients are purchased for freshness making a variety of flavors of IPAs, stouts, and ales with hundreds of malt choices, and several different types of yeast. Within each batch, it's possible to re-harvest yeast using it up to 12 times, or so. It's measured by staining it blue and viewed under a microscope to reveal if it is live and reusable. "The process becomes even more complicated after deciding on yeast strains making either ale or lager." Ron emphasizes, "you'd see a majority of craft brewers around San Diego developing ales, varying types of yeast feeding either top to the bottom for IPAs and ales, or bottom feeding to the top, and main characteristic of lager beers. As beer wort is fermenting, yeast is forming 'pacmen-type colonies' eating and digesting sugars and releasing CO_2 and alcohol."

The standard "Big Beer" popular brands contain higher alcoholic percentages because more grain adds more sugars in the brewing process. Ron elaborates, "the ales brewed with more flavors are wholly dependent on varieties of which yeast and malt are used, and all yeast strains are different with their level of tolerance and sustaining lifecycle. Certain yeasts can handle a lot of heat manufacturing alcohol while others may fall dormant sooner. And so, because there are multiple strains of yeast and multiple types of malted ingredients and hops; each recipe affects the outcome accordingly. Even the water must be filtered the right way for the best taste and depending on the system, the water adds varying tastes from minerals."

Enzymes are present within the germinated malted grains breaking down the complex simple sugars within a stainless kettle named the mashtun. It's filled with water and grains like barley, wheat, oats, or rye making a mixture using heated water at an appropriate temperature and brewing recipes naturally, until a solid mass forms in the middle. Jay remarks that at Prohibition Brewing, "during the boiling process we add hops and depending when you add hops determines how much bitterness and how much flavor you're going to get. Adding hops earlier gives more bitterness and contributes to enhanced flavor and aroma."

With the process nearing completion in the brew kettle, the brewer begins spinning the "wort" into a whirlpool recirculating the beer so all proteins and waste gather as "trub," a big solid mass in the middle. The whirlpool procedure clarifies liquid wort, the first unfermented brew, and wort is cooled through a heat exchanger, then transferred to the conical shaped fermenter adding oxygen and yeast. Once the yeast absorbs the oxygen it converts the sugar in CO_2 and alcohol." Ron's goal of brewing consistency draws repeat customers expecting the same fresh quality and balanced taste. He distributes throughout San Diego,

A relaxing stopover in Vista, Prohibition Brewery's speakeasy style reveals a fully furnished roadhouse serving great food and award winning craft beers, with plenty of parking.

HOURS
Kitchen closes 1 hour
before closing time
Mon-Thurs: 11-10pm
Fri: 11-11pm
Sat: 9-11pm
Sun: 9-10pm

Riverside, Temecula, as well as into Orange County. As demand is growing, the brewery's increasing reputation has stood apart from many others. Recently, Ron has reoccupied Fallbrook Brewing's spot in the Avocado Capital of the World. He now serves visitors from Prohibition Brewing taps at 136 North Main Street his best local brews.

The craft movement's prestigious reputation at the forefront of "West Coast styled beer" continues gaining both national and worldwide attention. Prohibition Brewery's strategic location in North County San Diego is a veritable treasure in the rough, and Ron and Kathy Adams have created a destination noteworthy for its award-winning craft beer and great food menu. Prohibition Brewing opens its doors at 11am, and there's an array of down-to earth-brews, as well as tasty grilled salmon, tacos, burgers, salads, and appetizers with a true feeling of hospitality from its dedicated staff.

PROHIBITION BREWERY'S QUOTES FROM PROHIBITION DAYS

Prohibition is better than no liquor at all.
Will Rodgers

There's no such thing as good money or bad money.
There's just money. *Lucky Luciano*

Once during prohibition I was forced to live on
nothing but food and water. *WC Fields*

Sayings by *Al Capone*:
I don't even know what street Canada is on.

You can get much farther with a kind word and
a gun than you can with a kind word alone.

I have built my organization on fear.

I am like any other man. All I do is supply and
demand.

The history of the Prohibition Era and its famous characters is traced through various mementos visible inside the brewery in a colorful theme.

PURE PROJECT

9030 Kenamar Dr #308
San Diego, Ca 92121
858-252-6143

Bankers Hill
2865 Fifth Ave.
San Diego, CA 92103

Jesse Pine and Agi Pine, Founders
Winslow Sawyer, Brewer
Mat Robar, Media
www.purebrewing.org

After three years brewing organic craft beer in the tropical climate of Costa Rica, a new adventure brought Pure Project's team of Jesse and Agi Pine into the middle of San Diego's craft brewing world in 2015. It became a means introducing their concept brewing pure "farm in a glass" style beer and using locally sourced organically grown ingredients. During a meeting of minds, Agi and Jesse made a giant step starting a new brewery in Miramar signing with H.G. Fenton's "Brewery Igniter" program at the center of the craft beer revolution. Winslow Sawyer, formerly a brewer at Boulder Creek Brewing once operating near Santa Cruz, eagerly had moved to San Diego joining the craft beer team at Pure Project as the brew master and co-partner. Completing the team, Mat Robar joined to disseminate and market the team's incredible products. The opportunity had been deemed an incredible success from its head start leasing the pre-installed brewery equipment and H.G. Fenton's turnkey warehouse tasting room, the ideal location for Pure Project inside the San Diego craft brewing community.

Earning a Bronze Medal at the San Diego International Beer Festival in 2019, their American-Style Juicey or Hazy Pale Ale -Murklands represents an important new brewery class. Brewing consistently great beer, Pure Project pays strict attention to the quality of the ingredients. "We believe every beer should tell a story just like a world class meal, a perfect cup of coffee, or a timeless wine, and we aim to bring that same level of passion, creativity, and artistry to the ever-evolving craft beer community. We like sharing our art with the movement focusing on quality and experience giving context to the beer in your glass."

Lines form around the block at specially released beers from Pure Project in Miramar.

Of the beers, Pure Project's Milagro is a seasonally Dry Stout depending on the freshest harvests sourcing flavors organically from a Costa Rican coffee farm. Romeo + Julius, a cream ale features freshly infused Valencia oranges from a farm in Fallbrook delivering rich rewarding flavors. Delphyne, the Berliner-style Weiss beer is brewed with local dragonfruit, an anti-oxidant vitamin-rich cactus. Organic honey and fresh hops are supplied from Fallbrook and star propelling local craft of Pure Project Brewing to an immediate success. At a recent local hop harvest, a wet hop beer blended with organic Cascade, Horizon and Nugget hops became, Hop Whisperer. Now in their third year, the 7-bbl brew house uses four 15-barrel brite tanks and four 15-barrel uni tanks. The brewery's latest releases posted on the web draw swarms lining up around the block on release

days. There are Food Truck arrivals scheduled for each beer release party. The brewery offers several fresh six-pack can releases of the next generation of handcrafted brews naturally from Pure Project, in Miramar.

(Courtesy of Pure Project Brewing)

QUANTUM BREWING COMPANY

5375 Kearny Villa Road #116
San Diego, CA 92123
www.quantumbrewingsd.com
858-254-6481

Marin Beauleau, Ph.D. Owner / Head Brewer

Dr. Martin Beaulieu, a PhD scientist has given new life to an old brewery in the Kearny Mesa Clairemont area. Join visits at the brewery for scientific discussions, yoga and more.

It's easy to tell owner-brewmaster, Dr. Martin Beaulieu has breathed new life into Quantum Brewing Company's success story, after reopening the brewery in Summer, 2016. As a PhD scientist, Martin's educated approach to brewing beer was like applying the science of Einstein and Max Planck into his own inspirational brewing techniques, a brewing scientist in his own right! He invites visiting professors and scientists to Quantum's community gatherings for celebratory evenings honoring scientific events. Martin's lectures on science premieres with his own newly released beer specials. The results have earned mutual respect from customers enjoying iconic brewing concepts and intricately crafted beers. Each choice is aptly labeled with an appropriate theme. Artistically crafting beer has become a driving passion. "Today, I'm gaining an increased sense of confidence in the possibilities." Martin recounts, "Our

Quantum gatherings include science, social, and community holidays at the brewery. Located in Kearny Mesa, it is easily found exiting Hwy 163 intersection and Clairemont Mesa Rd.

Solar Flare appeared freshly brewed during our observation of the recent solar eclipse." It was a creation of complex flavors, and soon the beer vanished into totality while the solar event was being viewed on the brewery's 100-inch screen. Martin's impressive scientific knowledge of brewing applies to his own scientific background in biotech. Visitors to the brewery may find as many as 12 beers any day of the week. He's naturally an inspired tinkerer crafting great beers. Local enthusiasts recently joined in overwhelming approval attending his first anniversary in August 2017. He regularly produces weekly specialties for avid customers arriving daily testing the latest 'New Age' beer at the brewery. Quantum Brewery's determination and spark of genius making complex tastes at the brewery taps earns Martin many lasting customer relationships.

Martin's brewing interests began in 2012 inspired by an extensive training in chemistry. Martin's commitment to the natural sciences remains a dedicated and central theme in his daily life. Quantum's mastermind explains, "sugar extractions made from malt are a biochemical reaction leaving you in control of the beer's body feel. I think I have a keen edge with my interest in biochemistry, just with malt! It is fascinating, it is great! There's infinite number beers you can make…generally you use barley, oats, rye, or rice, although there are a few I've

(Courtesy of Quantum Brewing)

not tried yet but any grain may be malted."

The brewery has become a very busy place open at 12 noon everyday, with the taps working daily. Martin Beaulieu's brewing ritual becomes transformational working with his hands. It's a stark contrast to the heady world of biotech science versus today's brewing laboratory. His former home once in Quebec and leaving for a position in the U.S., he and his wife decided moving to San Diego, and it's been Canada's loss and our gain ever since. During a recent nature walk in the highlands of northern San Diego County near Mount Palomar, Martin mused, "it's inspiring taking in the Spring wildflower season and having a once-in-a-lifetime experience seeing and photographing vast colors of California poppy blooms at their peak. The most natural settings are a means to new ideas. Natural surroundings have inspired recipes keeping customers happy anytime at Quantum Brewery." Thankfully, Martin's skills are at the center of the West Coast craft beer scene. The taproom presents visitors with an honorary commemorative wall of ovations observing Martin's passion for many great scientists. The pub's pervasive aura of theoretical possibilities will inspire you, the moment you enter. Brewing craft beer in 3-barrel batches creates ongoing living works of art each time. Quantum Brewing has stainless growlers on hand in the barroom keeping many happy aficionados returning. Ultimately for craft beer, "It's the place to watch for what you wish!"

In Santee, CA, Pacific Islander Brewing opens its door and Hawaiian patio each day in 'Mahalo' friendship for the enjoyment of its customers.

Modern Times Brewery & Restaurants began September, 2013, in North Park, and since establishing stores from LA County, all the way to Portland, Oregon.

Located at 3038 University Ave, San Diego, brewer, Kelsey McNair, established the North Park Beer Co. as a sophisticated brewery showcasing craft beer in 2016.

The iconic Stone Brewing tasting room in Oceanside reflects an upscale, earthy theme with a touch of elegance throughout each of their San Diego breweries.

Rip Current Brewing

1325 Grand Ave., Suite 100
San Marcos, CA 92078
760-481-3141

Rip Current North Park
4101 30th St.
San Diego, CA 92104
619 793-4777
www.ripcurrentbrewing.com

Paul Sangster, Owner / Brewmaster
Guy Shobe, Owner
Justin Stambaugh, Head Brewer

Paul Sangster recalled his first brewing days well before opening Rip Current Brewing in 2012. "It was a whole different world in 1992, when I first began brewing my own beer. I was using convenient off the shelf products. Later on, a friend wanted me to meet a challenge using barley grain malts instead of extracts, not so long ago, in 2007." Paul's fascination brewing craft beer emanated from a methodical scientific software engineering background. "I worked from my home in Carlsbad and worked brewing every weekend to create beer for competition."

(Courtesy of Rip Current Brewing Co.)

Paul's career as a brewer began in earnest joining Quaff, and the North County's Society of Barley Engineers, both locally organized San Diego home brewer clubs. Paul built camaraderie with other members started drawing acclaim for his prolific brewing skills. He made constant progress and enrolled in the BJCP, a certification program for beer judges focusing on the brewing elements of traditional examples of all 23 beer styles. Paul entered many blind tasting competitions and in particular focusing on the America's Finest City competition in San Diego. He won the most medals than anyone all the years between 2009-2011, winning the "Brewing Machine" award. Later, he entered three of the most important home brew competitions in California. Paul won the most overall medals resulting in the noteworthy award as the "Sierra Nevada California Homebrewer of the Year" in 2011. Finally entering the American Homebrewer Association's most prestigious home brew competition in the world, he again won the most medals and crowned with the prestigious "Ninkasi Award", and "Top Homebrewer in the World".

Recent winnings at 2019's San Diego International Beer Festival include a Bronze Medal for their European Lager, High Surf Helles, a Gold Medal win for an Amber Lager, Corriente Negra Mexican Lager, and a Gold Medal for a German-Style Bock, Breakline Bock; and previously in 2018, Silver Medals for Choppy Surf Czech Pilsner, and the German Style Bock, Breakline Bock. Topping off the event won a coveted Gold Medal awarded for their German Style Bock, Delaminator Doppelbock. At the Great American Beer Festival in 2019, their Bronze Rescue Buoy Imperial Stout won a Bronze Medal. Home brewing club member, Guy Shobe had mastered many traditional styles, as well. Guy was brewing on his own over the years and found the hobby a creative process appealing to his engineering side to technically craft a perfect beer. Together with Paul, and in partnership with two others, Rip Current Brewing in San Marcos opened on December 5, 2012. The brewery concept was based on a common San Diego theme. And, although "Rip Tide" was really a misused misnomer pulling swimmers out to sea, the team chose "Rip Current"

representing the awesome force of the ocean matching their own beer. San Diego's interconnectivity between brewers, beer judging and home brewing expertise has brought Rip Current's plans into fruition. Legendary Quaff member, Harold Gulbransen, would impart important technical feedback hitting target recipes creating each beer style. Also Quaff emeritus, Peter Zien, San Diego's only Grand Master Level 1 Judge contributed guidance towards Paul's achievement becoming San Diego's second certified Level 1 Master Judge.

Rip Current's San Marcos brewery's 7,000 sq. ft. facility is visible from the Hop Highway 78, and features equipment outfitted by Premier Stainless, a specialist in nearby Escondido. The team at Rip Current decided configuring their custom 15-barrel brewing system to meet the highest standards possible. Instead of a single burner fired under the kettle, Paul and Guy set up a powered system using a jacket of steam enveloping the wort. It adds accuracy controlling crucial temperatures in all brewing kettles. A brewer can adjust for more delicate flavors especially balancing out lighter color beers. Working on experimental pilot projects, Paul keeps the original all-grain 'More Beer' system he started out with years earlier. Another important concern at Rip Current Brewing is making a wide range of delicious styles by bringing attention to one main ingredient - the water formulation. As Paul describes, "we study the role of ions in the water when making a great IPA. Higher levels of sulfate ions naturally increases the crispness and brightness in taste. However, making a porter or stout and less bitter beer, you need higher chloride ions. San Diego's higher levels of sulfate ions occur naturally in the water, therefore many local IPAs are enhanced without checking the water scientifically. The point being you can't have it both ways making a sweeter finish beer without adjustment in water."

To be entirely accurate, the brewery employs RO, reverse osmosis rendering water inert then adding back the correct ionic flavor formula specific to each

Paul Sangster and Rip Current Brewery team at the brewery, located off Hop Highway 78, in San Marcos.

beer. Ions in water including calcium and magnesium are both important for yeast health. Sulfate, chloride, sodium bicarbonate and sodium carbonate are other important water ions.

It's exciting to know Rip Current earned the most desired award at the Great American Beer Festival in Denver, CO. The largest commercial beer competition in the world honored Rip Current Brewing, the 2015 "Very Small Brewing Company of the Year." Producing less than 1000 barrels annually, Rip Current won one of the highest number of medals in brewing competition. At 2017's San Diego International Beer Festival, Rip Current's Java Storm Coffee Imperial Stout was awarded a brilliant Gold Medal. Rip Current's Imperial Stout, Rescue Buoy Ris brought home a Bronze Medal. Also, Breakline Bock won a Silver Medal and Delaminator Doppelbock a Bronze Medal, both German-style Bock beers. Rip Current self-distributes to local tap rooms, restaurant accounts, also turns out cans, growler fills, and kegs. The brewery opened a second Rip Current brewery tasting room with a restaurant in North Park. The focus relies on pairing great craft beer with fresh quality food. The tasting room features over 15 taps serve freshly brewed quality beer. It's become a popular destination of craft beer and food enthusiasts in San Diego's downtown. Achieving and creating the best, Rip Current continues making award-winning beers and expanded with their North Park tasting room, drawing attention the brewery's highly regarded brewing expertise within today's crowded craft marketplace.

ROULEUR BREWING COMPANY

5840 El Camino Real Suite 101
Carlsbad, CA 92008
www.rouleurbrewing.com
442-244-5111

Rawley Macias, Head Rouleur

A neighborhood brewery in Carlsbad, brewery owner, Rawley Macias, developed and designed his brewery with the H.G. Fenton Brewery Igniter Program.

Rawley Macias brings a scientific engineer's enthusiasm to a newly established brewery in Carlsbad. His ability as a brewer became a deciding factor visualizing a successful custom microbrewery complimenting his natural curiosity towards the skills mastering great craft beer. There had been challenges to home brewing in his early 20s that were far from a tedious career in aerospace living in San Luis Obispo. Enrolled as a qualified beer judge according to the highest standards of BJCP certification, he began experimenting with new beer formulas and unique blends home brewing over 12 years. He began creating something special. Moving to North County San Diego and finding his own place among the craft beer movement, Rouleur Brewing joined a growing brewery trend featuring proprietary blends and specialty beers. The brewery became part of the third H.G. Fenton Brewery Igniter, a leasing program based in San Diego. Tucked into a quiet industrial park in central Carlsbad, Rouleur Brewing Co. opened a pre-designed turnkey brewery featuring an installed

10-barrel Premier brewing system with a 100-gallon cellar capacity ready for its first batch. The Brewery Igniter represents a brewer's dream towards moving a career into high gear. The company assembles the entire brewery, so it's ready to occupy. The Rouleur Brewing Company's Grand Opening on April 8, 2017 moved Rawley's enterprising goals into high gear as the next North County neighborhood destination brewery. Today at Rouleur, there are kegs, growler fills and proprietary draft beer on tap.

In 2019, Rawley's Gold Medal win for his American-Style Pale Ale, BONKEUR Mosaic Pale Ale, was backed up by a Bronze Medal for his Hybrid Belgian-Style Ale, PUNCHEUR Pale Ale, and a Silver Medal for a Belgian-Style Pale Ale, DOMESTIQUE Blonde Ale, another Silver Medal for a Belgian-Style Pale Strong Ale, SOLOIST Golden Strong Ale at the 2019 San Diego International Beer Festival. Rawley's career as a certified judge at beer competitions lasted only a couple of years after aspirations of realizing craft beer beyond the restrictive age-old traditions of common styles. Beer judges rate beer according to certain targets, and they even berate home brew styles if they stray away from a specific mouth feel, flavor, color, or formula. Rawley began creating hybrid ales born from traditional American ale styles of grain malts and hops, yet exclusively brewed with a subtle Belgian yeast strain. The beer he makes adds incredibly natural tastes and flavors. Setting Rouleur's core beers ahead of the standard, and the styles are named succinctly according the Head Rouleur's Blonde, Golden Strong, Red Ale, Pale Ale, IPA, Double IPA and Stout. All beers are brewed using a European yeast imparting basic flavors from familiar western brewing ingredients. Yeast may dominate a beer's flavor depending on the formula and brewing methods. The 2018 San Diego International Beer Festival brought home a Bronze Medal for Rouleur's Hybrid Belgian, PUNCHEUR Pale Ale. From French, the name Rouleur infers "roller" or a pro cyclist prepared to meeting any challenge. The brewery's opening in 2017 has attracted Carlsbad's bike friendly community and adds to a growing local brewery tour, serving globally-styled beers conceived locally.

San Diego Brewing Co.

Grantville Brewery and Restaurant
10450 Friars Rd.,
San Diego, CA 92120
619-284-2739 (brew)
www.sandiegobrewing.com

Lee Doxiter, Owner
Scott Stamp, Owner

By the end of 1989, as home brewers making craft beer, Lee Doxtider and
Scott Stamp became acutely aware of San Diego's trending tastes for good beer
and great food. They established their original legendary brewpub that year,
Callahan's Pub & Brewery in Mira Mesa using a 3-barrel nano-brewing system.
The brewpub kept seven taps flowing into the night. At that point, Scott and
Lee decided researching the town's historical namesake brewery and finding it
available, San Diego Brewing Company was re-registered in their name. In 1993,
introducing the new company's beer, they stepped into the future of San Diego's
craft beer history, reopening the San Diego Brewing Company. Featuring
a 7-barrel brewery and brewpub restaurant in the historical Mission Valley
neighborhood, their location was established on Friar's Road near San Diego's
first Spanish mission.

They instantly gained recognition on the craft scene having on hand an amazing
50 taps. It was more than anyone had conceived previously and they included
choices of many local labels. Today, they are serving local craft beer selections,
ready to pair with great food. The core San Diego Brewing's finest award-
winning beers include San Diego Gold®, San Diego Amber®, and San Diego
IPA®. Lee and Scott formed a partnership and established a new brewery
in North Park under H.G. Fenton's CRAFT Brewery Igniter program. The
brewery increased production and retired the original Callahan's brewpub after
serving customers nearly 28 years. Today, the team focuses solely on their San
Diego brewery, and Lee and Scott have earned the highest regards from fellow
brewers, as well as accumulating a long list of award-winning San Diego beer,
most recently earning a Silver Medal at 2017's San Diego International Beer
Festival for Welter Wit, a Belgian-style Wit or White Ale.

The history of the first San Diego Brewing Company was established by
the city's founding father Alonzo E. Horton, in 1896. Adding the financing
from John D. Spreckles, the brewery had grown to the largest manufacturing
industrial enterprise in early San Diego County. The vintage brewery site is now
a US Navy Naval Station at 32nd Street downtown, and the original brewery
once had relocated to the vintage Mission Brewery brick building at Hancock
and Washington Streets. With progressing modernity, in 1906 the brewery
upgraded its new refrigeration system operating a large 100-ton compressor.
They began switching horse-drawn delivery wagons to newer motor vehicles.
The brewery's annual output increased to 140,000 barrels a year. Beer deliveries
were being made all the way into San Francisco and Arizona. Later acquiring
the local Fredericksburg Brewery,and Mission Brewery in 1914, the company
reorganized into the San Diego Consolidated Brewing Company.

There was a 25-horsepower engine installed operating the elevator, barley mill
and mashtun in the historical heart of brewhouse. The brewery's fermenting
cellar's capacity stored 75,000 barrels. However, the brewery's success was
paralleled with a looming plight restricting "dry cities" and supporting
prohibition nationally. The unstoppable wave in California's towns and
cities had crested at the turn of the century brought on by the temperance
movement. Some breweries and saloons were forced into closure well before
1919's momentum ratifying the Prohibition Amendment and a completing the
demise of commercial brewing nationally in 1920. The old San Diego Brewing
Company remained brewing "near beer" called Hopski, bottling it out of the
landmark Mission Brewery building into the mid-1920s. With the onset of
WWII and national attention focused on war, San Diego's namesake brewing
company passed into history in 1942.

Fast forward 50 years into the future and a old vibrant craft name is now
resurrected from obscurity. San Diego Brewing Company is preserved by
Lee Doxtider and Scott Stamp following a successful but narrow path from
1989. Abundant rewards and great notoriety has followed San Diego Brewing
Company's tasty preparations of fresh food and craft beer for all to enjoy!

The original San Diego Brewpub off Friars Road, is a popular tap room and tradition in San Diego early in the rise of craft breweries in San Diego.

Select award-winning brews at San Diego International Beer Festival competitions representing San Diego Brewing's the highest quality:

2019	Helles For Children …European Lager	Silver
2016	Pale in Drop D …Bitter	Bronze
2016	San Diego IPA …American-style India Pale Ale	Gold
2014	San Diego Amber …American-style Amber/Red Ale	Silver
2014	Grantville Gold …German-style Ale	Silver
2013	80 Schilling …Scottish-style Ale	Bronze
2013	Lakshmi Imperial Red …Imperial Red Ale	Bronze
2010	Hopnotic …Double IPA	Silver
2010	San Diego Amber …Amber Hybrid Beer	Gold
2009	Callahan's Blueberry Wheat …Fruit Beer	Bronze
2009	Callahan's Red …American Amber and Brown Ale	Bronze
2007	ChocolaLatte Porter …Spice/Herb/Vegetable Beer	Bronze
2007	Aztec Gold …Light Hybrid Beer	Bronze
2007	Old Town Brown …English Brown Ale	Bronze

New English Brewing's large gathering space is available for parties and receptions in Sorrento Mesa. (Courtesy of New English Brewery).

Vivid colorful graphics at the Novo Brazil's brewery building offers plenty of room to make a perfect countryside getaway visit to southeast Chula Vista.

Second Chance Beer Co.

Brewery & Tap Room
15378 Avenue of Science Suite 222
San Diego, CA 92128
858-705-6250

Second Chance Beer Lounge
North Park Tasting Room
4045 30th St., Suite A
San Diego, CA 92104
619-487-1470
www.secondchancebeer.com

Marty Mendiola, Brewmaster/Co-founder
Virginia Morrison, Renaissance Woman/Co-founder
Curtis Hawes, Chief Tasting Officer/Co-founder
Craig Gregovics, Head Brewer

Marty Mendiola became one of San Diego's first professional craft brewers led by a driving passion for brewing great craft beer over 17 years ago. He became a GABF Gold Medal award-winner in 2009, known for his English-style Brown Ale, Longboard Brown. At 2018's San Diego International Beer Festival, Second

Chance won a brilliant Gold Medal honoring their Red Ale, Mulligan Irish-Style Red. A recent 2019 Gold Medal win for Marty's Tabula Rosa for a California Robust Porter, is a testament to his earliest work experience at Karl Strauss Brewing Company in San Diego's downtown, and he graduated with a Masters in Brewing Arts at UC Davis. Upon graduation, Rock Bottom Brewing Co. in Denver, Colorado offered him his first professional brewing position. A few years later, Marty became Head Brewer in La Jolla at Rock Bottom Brewery showcasing recipes he had developed. He released many tasty beer styles over the next fifteen years and aware of the craft beer movement gaining stature, Marty began planning with Curtis Hawes, Rock Bottom's assistant general manager about starting Second Chance Beer Co. Marty with his future wife and attorney, Virginia Morrison had in place all the requirements needed operating a successful brewery. The Grand Opening of Second Chance Brewing in September 2015, began a bright new future for Marty and Virginia, Curtis, and Greg Gregovics, the company's first employee. Look for Second Chance Beer Co., "So Happy It's Thursday Weekly Releases" featuring bourbon barrel-aged beers, cutting edge infusions, and creative sours at the tasting rooms. Virginia considers the fortunate moments from the beginning, "a very prominent brewer gave us our first yeast and generally is not approachable by anyone. We also used a secondary market supplied by local brewer friends selling grain overages they've kept in storage."

Virginia elaborates Second Chance Beer's goals, "we enjoy serving IPAs but not the resiny oily dank kind. We brew many 6% abv session beers, English Brown, Irish Red, Robust Porter, Belgian-style Golden Ale, not quads and triples. There are nine of sixteen taps serving English session style beers. Our Jalapeño

& Lime Infused Blonde Ale and other creations are on rotation. Practically, everyone comes to Second Chance finding a beer they'd enjoy. Marty prefers more balanced beers, so we make a lot of traditional styles but add a nuance of natural flavor at times. We use real fruits, real nuts, even organic blueberries from local partners. One example that became our July 4th release and guest favorite is made with real blueberries and raspberries infused into a wonderful saison, Red, White and Blue Beery."

The Rock Bottom Brewery chain consists of 30 brewpubs nationally, and Marty became a Senior Brewer meriting virtually unfettered discretion brewing his own beer and formulating award-winning recipes competitively during a seventeen year career there. Second Chance Beer Co. was derived from Marty and Virginia's budding romance and Curtis's long friendship as a stepping stone into the successful local, independent San Diego craft brewery it is today. As Virginia explains, "a second chance is a way of making the most from an opportunity when there's an inspired feeling to be successful while giving back." Regarding customers Virgina muses, "we are excited about reaching people who don't like beer, and often they'll come back for brewery events or monthly fundraisers, and I'll see them becoming fans. Visitors already know about us in China and Portugal through local hotels serving our beer. It's really a grass roots marketing effort."

The Second Chance theme follows repurposing all opportunities and has worked well for the brewery furniture and decor. Most items are donated, reclaimed, and refinished. The curious-looking handmade decorative lighting fixtures are wooden barrel staves. Virginia explains, "even the baseboards in the brewery are recycled fencewood from the house Marty grew up in! We reinvent to bring objectivity to our busy surroundings "second chance" things not only because it's consistent with our company values, but also because we hope it will inspire our guests and others to think about ways they can do the same. When Rock Bottom closed their downtown location, we salvaged their tables and restored them. The legs came from construction discards. Our friends at Lost Abbey donated old barrels after aging their famous beer, and we power-washed and incorporated them as part of the brewery's bar."

Teaming up Second Chance with community causes and local charities offers a chance to give back. Virginia explains, "One fundraiser, Donate Life San Diego, providing the ultimate gift to people receiving donated organs and tissues for a second chance at life. We have had fundraisers for animal rescue programs, local residents battling cancer, community school Foundations, and FixIt Clinics, and to keep stuff out of landfills. One of our beers, Brewbies On My Mind, supports Keep A Breast Foundation, an organization dedicated to breast cancer prevention, year round. Also, joining 20 other breweries, we've contributed to supporting our friends diagnosed with Lupus and a organization led by a local journalist, 'Beer to the Rescue' was created for funding the Lupus Foundation in San Diego."

People come to Second Chance and take guitar lessons offered twice per month, or spend time playing darts, Cornhole and board games in the family friendly atmosphere. The brewery recently opened a new North Park Tasting Room with 1,820 sq. ft. with 24 taps and an outdoor patio at 4045 30th Street. The brewery extends a welcome to all its guests with the idea that a second chance, generally is, "the ultimate expression of opportunity –although we may not all get one, and if you do, seize it!"

Find the brewery and tap room on Avenue of Science, in the Carmel Mountain neighborhood not far from the Black Mountain Open Space Park with 2,352 acres of hills, ridges and canyons for hiking and biking. There's a central peak offering a 360-degree view. It's good to know at Second Chance, "there are FOOD TRUCKS at the brewery almost every night and with 3,500 square feet of tap room goodness, that means there's plenty of room for everyone you know."

SMOKING CANNON BREWERY

780 Main Street, Unit 1
(Entrance on 8th Street)
Ramona, CA 92065
760-407-7557
www.smokingcannonbrewery.com

NatallieRose Phillips, Co-founder / CEO, Brewer
Mike Nelson, Co-founder / Brewer

Natallie Phillips and Mike Nelson

Whether savoring a flight of tasters or full pint – Smoking Cannon Brewery's craft beers are infused with brewing passion one-step beyond the ordinary! The founders of Smoking Cannon Brewery, Natallie Phillips and Mike Nelson, tested the waters and made historical Ramona their home over 20 years ago. A devoted partnership in life, they've shared San Diego's tradition of brewing great craft beer without extracts and using fresh ingredients. An equal opportunity community pub for young and old, Smoking Cannon is also the perfect stop for refreshing non-alcoholic in-house craft drinks, including ginger beer, or root beer from time-tested recipes, and a smooth Papua New Guinea Cold Brew coffee served on nitro. Smoking Cannon Brewery's location is known as a vibrant downtown family friendly center in the midst of Ramona's eclectic antique shops and authentic Mexican restaurants. As brewing partners, the duo is no stranger to competition recently earning two professional medals at the 2019 New York International Beer Festival. They won a Bronze for Natallie's German Chocolate Cake Milk Stout called Joslyn, as well as finishing first place with a Gold Medal win as the "Best Chocolate Brewery" in California. Consistently, Mike has delivered multiple decades of numerous

The Eighth Street Brewery Entrance is just around the corner of Main St., in Ramona.

award-winning home brews of many medals. Visitors to the brewery may choose from 10 basic beers, or growler fills are available – backed by the team's awesome award-winning background. There have been many brewing successes with unique varieties and styles; including Kentucky Common, one of few true American beers found on tap, and more familiar in the Eastern states. The original recipe dates back to before the Civil War and made with true Kentucky Whiskey mash, with American two row, flaked corn and rye malt. Among flagship beers at the brewery, recent winners at the LA Beer Festival included bringing a Silver Medal for a bold American Stout, Coehorn, served on tap with smooth nitro, or regular CO_2; and, another brewery favorite named Paxton, their Smoked Peanut Butter Ale earned a Bronze Medal. The brewery's tangy American IPA was dubbed Parrott; a lighter Blond Ale called Cyrus; as well as, each Smoking Cannon beers are borrowed names from their antique 19th century artillery counterparts, and – the BIGGER the cannon, the BIGGER the beer.

"Our Chili beer, Blakely, reflects the brewery's southern location, brewed directly with raw Anaheim and roasted Anaheim Chilies and Paseo's 'Ancho' chilis." As Natallie explains, "It's not a hot beer, but when paired with enchiladas it adds an especially crisp natural flavor to the food. Chili beer is the main component to our refreshing 'Micheladas' added with around 1/4 Bloody Mary mix to a pint of beer. If you like spice, then we add Habanero chili for peak flavors."

Mike's creations include a working 1/3 size model Howizter Civil War cannon. See it and others at the brewery.

Once inside the brewery, the laid back interior and historical backdrop lends to an "after the war is over" theme, and a perfect place to relax and meet community folks. The brewery's tastefully arranged wood-trim gallery walls are covered with sepia-toned portraits depicting vintage Civil War artillery namesakes of the beers, topped by a perimeter of historical flags in honor of our colorful American past. Mike's youthful years had revealed many historic battlefields down south and fascinating Civil War stories. In addition to his trade as a welder, he began a hobby of machining real cannon that actually fire, an art that eventually led to the brewery's name.

After starting life in San Diego, the team decided relocating to Ramona between the towns Julian and Escondido, and well above the fray of San Diego freeways and traffic lights. In the small town of Ramona, just off today's Hop Highway 78 East, the brewery is surrounded largely by ranches and farms at 1,500 ft. elevation and features a sprawling downtown kaleidoscope of conveniences. Mike and Natallie spotted the perfect locale for a Main Street address, and today's professional brewery opened its doors, May 13, 2017. Public access is just off Main, at the 8th Street entrance. Spending an entire year resurrecting the building's interior setting the brewery up from scratch, today's location reflects the team's elegant vision of being among the best in San Diego. To top off the many hours of renovations behind them, Mike created his own new 3-barrel electric brewing system, hand fabricating all the stainless components to his own specifications. The brewery is a star attraction, as well as today's only small craft brewery operating in Ramona today. Running the brewery has met the team's personal goals aimed at serving their community in as many ways possible. Starting from the brewery's appearances at the town festivals and charity events, they often introduce their craft beers to folks from San Diego's neighboring suburbs… for which, the historical town of Ramona is most grateful.

SOCIETE BREWING COMPANY

8262 Clairemont Mesa Blvd.
San Diego, CA 92111
858-598-5409
www.societebrewing.com

Douglas Constantiner, Co-founder / CEO
Travis Smith, Co-founder / Brewmaster

"Community is everything, especially in craft beer. Beer is a big part of society's breaking down barriers, and beer is for everyone in society," explains Travis Smith, brewmaster at Societe Brewing Co. From 2004-09, an early association at Russian River Brewery's Santa Rosa brewpub had an enormous influence on Travis. He was brewing diverse beer styles at one of the most highly respected breweries in the Golden State. His career later led to joining The Bruery in Orange County, where he met Doug Constantiner. Through camaraderie and communications, they had found a solid unity forming San Diego's Societe Brewing Company in 2011. As Doug points out, "some of the best beers in the world cost just $5, so they are accessible. We're honored by the advice San Diego's bigger, older craft breweries share with us smaller guys." Between avid home brew clubs, fundraising events, competitions, a strong Brewer's Guild, and social media, Societe Brewing effectively is interconnected to San Diego's mainstream. Doug emphasizes, "Likewise, as we grow our brewing community,

we cannot be end-users. If you're lucky enough to have information shared with you, you should be willing to share it with others." Through the patio gate and front door, Societe's spaciously designed tasting room reveals a perfect place to enjoy beer and have a conversation with others. The concept is clearly defined by Societe's comfortably arranged seating and tasting room bar surrounded by earthy knotty pine paneling offsetting the brewery's shiny tank farm. Silhouetted caricatures and nostalgic imagery carry the brewery theme to the tasting room's unique beer styles. A logical thing about Societe Brewing Co. are clear definitions of their beer classified as: Out West, Old World, Stygian, or bottled Feral ales. Core beers featured year 'round are about one-third of the taps and rotated as the team brews batches of newly released beer.

At the 2019 San Diego International Beer Festival, judged by the beer's class, Societe's brewing prowess handily obtained five medals that included a Gold Medal win for a Hybrid Belgian-Style Ale, The Harlot; another Gold Medal for their European Lager, The Baroness; a Silver Medal for a Brett and other Sour Beer, The Highwayman; a Bronze Session Beer, The Coachman; and a Bronze Medal for Brett and other Sour Beer, The Swindler. Out West explores the potential of hop-forward West Coast styles. Bringing the highest honors at the Great American Beer Festival (GABF) in 2015, The Coachman earned a coveted Gold Medal for best Session IPA. The Apprentice, Societe's American-Style Pale Ale won a Silver Medal in 2013 for their Strong-style Pale Ale. And a house favorite, The Pupil IPA won a Bronze Medal in the International-style

Pale Ale category at the 2014 GABF. It was highly honored as San Diego's Best at the 2013 Blind Lady Ale House's Blind IPA Challenge. Stygian beer radiates deep cavernous tones known for stouts and dark lagers. Societe's Gold Medal for their Imperial Stout, The Butcher was honored at 2013's San Diego International Beer Festival. Its well-balanced dark roasted malt flavors combining a densely cocoa-covered head with French Roast accents. At 2016's GABF, Societe's The Volcanist, an American Stout earned a Bronze Medal. Many newly introduced beers are released at the brewery, often entered into blind tasting competitions at a later date. Societe's classic Irish-style Dry Stout, The Pugilist, a dark dry session stout with a 4.5% abv had been awarded 2014's Silver Medal at the prestigious World Beer Cup. Perhaps, the most interesting are Societe's Old World traditional beer brewed with West Coast flair. One example, The Harlot brought the brewery a Bronze Medal for a Hybrid Belgian-style Ale at San Diego's International Beer Festival in 2017. At 2018's San Diego International Beer Festival, Societe Brewing's Belgian Pale Ale, The Damsel, was awarded a Silver Medal, a mark of consistency at the brewery. Ferals, are Societe's active barrel-aging program featuring beer sours with wild yeast and barrel-blended ales released in corked and caged bottles. The Highwayman Pale Ale is aged with brettanomyces, and there's limited supply of The Urchin infused with cranberries making a brilliant ale matured in red wine oak barrel tannin. The Urchin became part of a 2016 fundraiser for the San Diego Food Bank helping raise 24,000 lbs. of donated food. Easily accessed from several freeways connecting to Clairemont Mesa Blvd., the brewery is open at noon every day to the public, 7 days a week, child and family friendly. They allow dogs with a leash asking only they be well-behaved and well-supervised. There are well chosen food trucks arriving with specialty food pairings six days a week listed on the brewery's website. It's been pure inspiration for Doug working together with Travis and building the brewery. In their view, "Societe Brewing's Tasting Room was designed to serve craft beer in its ideal form – fresh from the brewery sitting 30 feet away. Not every beer is for you, but I guarantee there is a beer out there you will like." Travis and Doug are in agreement, "knowing and meeting our local residents and long time customers at Societe Brewing."

Independent San Diego brewery tasting and tap rooms are popular stops found on Claremont Mesa Blvd., near I-5.

Societe Brewing Co. offers spacious seating and an array of brewing equipment in the background. They feature several award-winning Old World and West Coast styles, sours and barrel-aged beers.

Karl Strauss brewpub at 1044 Wall St., La Jolla, serves American bar food with a gourmet twist and house-brewed craft ales.

From Judd McGhee's container collection at Citizen Brewers displays a few of San Diego's past labeled best beers.

STONE BREWING CO.

Stone Brewing World Bistro & Gardens
1999 Citracado Parkway
Escondido, CA 92029
760-294-7866

Stone Brewing World Bistro & Gardens
Liberty Station
2816 Historic Decatur Road
San Diego, CA 92106
619-269-2100

Stone Company Store - On Kettner
1202 Kettner Blvd., Ste.101
San Diego, CA 92101
619-450-4518

Stone Company Store - Oceanside
310 N. Tremont St.
Oceanside, CA 92054
760-529-0002

Stone Brewing Tap Room
795 J Street
San Diego, CA 92101
619-727-4452

Stone Company Store - Richmond
4300 Williamsburg Ave.
Richmond, VA 23231
804-489-5902

Stone Brewing Terminal 2 Gate 36
San Diego International Airport
San Diego, CA 92101
760-294-7899

Stone's Gothic iconography conjures a mythical era of gargoyles, dragon slayers, and monumental kingdoms paralleling a present day vision of a legendary brewing empire spread across the globe. Stone Brewing Co. rejects all normal protocol, "warding off cheap ingredients, pasteurization, and chemical additives, the modern-day evil spirits of beer!" Owners and co-founders, Greg Cook and Steve Wagner have indelibly forged their mark on craft brewing's future. A 2018 entry, Totalitarian Imperial Russian Stout, was a recent Bronze Medal winner at the San Diego International Beer Festival. There's little doubt Stone's legendary beer possesses symbolic notoriety as a leader in "The Capital of Craft" movement in San Diego and mirroring the company's success story clearly defining the role of West Coast craft beer, both nationally and worldwide. It's evident Stone holds its own as a fierce competitor against "Big Beer's" bland tasteless products maintaining several fully-owned craft breweries and taking a consistently positive stand.

Stone Brewing World Bistro & Gardens at Liberty Station combines massive stonework with elegant furnishings for meeting space, dining and beer tasting.

The visible brewery workings in full view at Stone's Escondido World Bistro & Gardens restaurant and tap room.

Stone's Escondido World Bistro & Gardens restaurant and tap room.

Comprehending Stone Brewing's vast empire in San Diego begins with six separate locations. Sophistication of design elements align all the breweries award-winning beer and farm fresh food as a full immersion and personalized experience. Liberty Station and Escondido's World Bistro & Gardens in San Diego each offer comfort zone settings of restaurants, gardens, and patio venues within an industrial sized brewery. All of Stone Brewing's classic restaurants serve "farm to table" fresh flavors. The Escondido brewery's lush bistro garden accommodates banquets, meetings, and delicious beer pairings. The brewery's dining room pours 36 craft specialty beers on tap and adds a distinctive wine list and garden fresh food from local farmsteads and Stone's own organic gardens. A wall of glass transitions the main brewery to the tap room into the restaurant's interior onto the meandering labyrinth one-acre garden outdoors.

Brewery tours may be arranged at San Diego's Escondido headquarters, as well as at the Richmond, Virginia and German breweries, and each are open daily to the public. The brewery's fresh beer is available nearly anywhere in California, as well as many distant localities. As a local label, Stone overcame obstacles unlocking its invincible force of craft excellence dominating the field. Achieving the highest award-winning excellence brewing craft beer and beer styles, Stone tapped into a niche very few world-esteemed innovative breweries occupy. The brewery's equipment often helps pilot new brews, as well as competitive trials among it's own and other brewers. It's an obvious alignment with the brewery's coalition in the local community. First established in a relatively small North County warehouse in 1996, craft consciousness led to stern resistance towards flagrant commercialization. Stone became a leader distinctly brewing a kaleidoscopic array of the highest possible fresh quality beer.

Stone launched a refreshing Tangerine Express IPA in six-packs with 12 oz. cans. The beer has a light color, juicy and tropical flavors, and brewed with whole tangerine, and whole pineapple purees. The IPA is also available in 22oz. bottles. (Courtesy of Stone Brewing Co.)

Stone Seasonals

Limited to 3 releases of 2 beers annually, one seasonal and one imperial seasonal. The beer reflects flavors and styles best enjoyed during an intended timeframe. A few labels include: Vengeful Spirit, Mocha IPA, Ghost Hammer, Pataskala, India Pale Ale, Milk Stout, Xoccovez, Citrusy Wit, Americano Stout.

Special Releases

An evolving series of special releases meant as a reflection of Stone Brewing's drive to branch out, break convention, and celebrate the art of brewing. Look for the labels: Triple IPA Ruinten, So Cal Ruinten, S&P Revolver IPA, Coffee Milk Stout, Vanilla Began, Imperial Russian Stout, Old Guardian Dry-Hopped, Stone Saison, Dry Spiced Russian Stout, Old Guardian, Extra Hoppy.

Stone Enjoy By IPA Series

Freshness is a key component of many beers, and in Stone's view especially making big, citrusy, floral IPAs, Double IPAs. The series features 10 hops and a visibly pronounced date on the label.

Stone Collaborations

Humbly acknowledging other great brewers and home brewers, the series is set up for collaborative brewing, and started in 2008. The beers don't conform to preconceived styles and include ridiculous amounts of decadent, unfamiliar ingredients.

Stone Anniversary Ales & Invitational Beer Festival

These are an annual toast to each year and a charity event held in August each year. Over the years over 2 million dollars have been raised for donation to select charities.

Small Batch Series

Experimental beers, transforming them into unique variations of our legendary recipes. Recently bottled, most exclusive beers we have to offer and compares side-by-side what aging and souring a brew in a variety of wine and alcohol infused barrels can do to the original. Warning limited quantities.

Stone Berlin Groundbreaking collaborations
2014 launched the Stone Berlin GB Collaboration, offering fas to preorder
fourteen special beers that would be created with some of the biggest names
in craft brewing.

Stone Enjoy after Brett IPA Series
Bottle conditioned with Brett, needs cellaring for minimum of one year.
Enjoy after date printed on the label.

Stone Spotlight Series
Craft, by nature, is about inventiveness and creativity. Intra-brewing
competitions with two-person teams as a light-hearted experiment in battle
to see whose beer recipe will make from pilot brew to distributed sensation.

20th Anniversary Encore Series
Celebrates the milestone over the course of an entire year releasing favorite
beers from our history. Original recipes and bottle art, and looking back
on highlights from the past. On the way into a future filled with continued
creativity, passion and fun.

Stone Stochasticity Project
Ready for a new vocabulary word? No Happenstance or coincidence is
the natural result of stochasticity, a concept embraced by the special and
unpredictable series, exotic notions, ingredients and ideas coalesce.

Stone Vertical Epic Ales
Bottle conditioned ales specifically designed to be aged with bottle-
conditioning. The lineup was intended to be enjoyed in a "vertical" tasting—
starting with 02.02.02 and ending with 12.12.12. Within it you'd find each
is unique to its year of release. Each providing its own "twist & turn" in
the plot line. Each one released one year, one month and one day from the
previous year's edition.

BASTARD BREWING

Liquid Arrogance in a glass is by definition the primary reason for Arrogant Bastard Brewing being established. A product of Stone Brewing, the first Arrogant Bastard Ale was released to the world on November 1, 1997 and since, the unruly brew seemed worthy of a life on its own. The ale's unexpected results shattered "the glass ceiling" of craft products and generally persists elevating the status of West Coast craft beer. Arrogant Bastard Brewing has spun off on its own in 2015 from Stone Brewing's lineage of specialty beer and other true departures from mediocrity. An uncompromising celebration combines integrity, taste, and sophistication, aggressively great beer, specialty one-year and annual releases. Among them are Double Bastard, Lukcy Basartd, Bigger, Longer, Uncut and Depth-Charged.

Year 'round Arrogant Bastard brews, Wussie Arrogant Bastard Ale and Arrogant Bastard Bourbon Barrel-Aged Ale are released on tap, and in cans and bottles. The most exclusive beer has been available at the brewery only is now in bottles. There's a range of a dozen barrel-aged experiments, and legendary recipes using a variety of wine and spirit infused barrels. "Arrogant Bastard Hits the Road" benefits ebullient talented brewers and shared brewing recipes in collaboration with local charities. Brewing beer for charity helps out places like the Mississippi Valley Blues Society, Champaign County Humane Society, or Iowa's Flash Adolescent and Young Adult Cancer Research. A main recipient, Foster Care to Success, benefits America's College Fund for Foster Youth.

WILD BARREL BREWING COMPANY

692 Rancheros Drive
San Marcos, CA 92069
760-230-9205

Temecula Tasting Room
41493 Margarita Rd. Bldg 106
Temecula, CA 92591
www.wildbarrelbrewing.com

Chris White, President
Bill Sysak, CEO
Bill Sobieski, Director of Brewing Operations
Preston Weesner, Director of Barrel Operations

In San Marcos, it's a world of action at Wild Barrel Brewing adding a touch of craftsmanship and elegance to each beer. You'll find a courteous beertender willing to guide you through an array of great craft beers and fruit sours on tap, or provide crowlers, growlers, kegs and six-packs on the go to take home. A large seating capacity and cheery environment at the brewery blends nicely with a visual background of wood casks, colorful murals, photography shows, and choice of 24 beers on tap. And at Wild Barrel, there's a reason behind sharing their extensive brewing expertise and knowledge.

"I'm on the advisory board of San Diego State University, and over six years I taught entry level and an advanced 'Craft Beer Education Camp' course; as well as consulting 25 years with breweries and bars. Also, I made an alliance with Stone Brewing's Sour Fest that grew into the largest one of its kind." A well known personality within North County's brew circles, Bill Sysak, is often referred to as 'Doctor Bill' from his previous career in ER at Orange County's St. Joseph's Hospital. After working for Stone Brewing World Bistro and Gardens as their ambassador of food pairing, wine and beer marketing, Dr. Bill handled many of their exclusive event functions over seven years. His vision of a brewery tasting room in San Marcos brought together the Wild Barrel Brewing Company team including three other partners, each awesome technicians covering all aspects running a brewery smoothly.

"Considering where craft beer is going, it's perfect timing at Wild Barrel. I find that beer favoritism has shifted singularly towards its flavor, a personal element of exploration for many beer enthusiasts." Bill relaunched into new businesses around 2001, then following his instincts marketing beer in 2009, he began managing events at Stone's World Bistro & Gardens in Escondido, and their later expansion of food and beverage events at Liberty Station. He started assembling his own brewing team in 2017, conveniently locating Wild Barrel Brewing on the frontage along Hop Highway 78, then formally opening the brewery at the end of February, 2018.

Specialties craft beers and fruit sours at Wild Barrel Brewing are developed expressly for the West Coast's direct market for familiar styles, expanded into a full spectrum of crafted flavors. Just out of the gate, the team entered and won a Silver Medal for Not Last Year's Fruitcake Old Ale, at the San Diego International Beer Festival in 2019. Then, they took the Brewbies 10th Anniversary Peoples Choice for their sour, Nectarine Cherry Craft Beer. Their beer selections are as bold as West Coast IPAs, Hazy IPAs, Imperial Stouts, lighter Pilsners, and popular fruit kettle sours known as Weisse; or rather, 'Vice' according to Wild Barrel Brewing's terminology. "We have Belgium Wit, also a Bohemian Pilsner lager, and we brew a German Pils. You have to make beer that drives customers to you."

Dr. Bill further elucidates on the role of his partners at the brewery and the Temecula Tasting Room. "Our company started with the entrepreneur of several companies, Chris White; and together with Bill Sobieski, who spent many years as a master homebrewer and member of Quaff and Barley Engineers. We've recently added Preston Weesner to our brewing team, who is known as the mastermind of 'Cascades Explosion' up in Portland with their sour beers." Defining the latest mission as, "an immensely popular program we dub 'Imperial Pastry Sours' meant to mimic tasty desserts, the brewery created their latest jewels, White Chocolate Raspberry Torte, a Peach Cobbler, and a green beer, Key Lime Pie, using spirulina; each beer as delicious as its counterpart pastry. Our kettle sours program is driving our market right now, and overseas we have a strong following in China, Japan, Vietnam and Australia. We use cold-chain distribution all the way, and we fulfill a constant demand."

Inside the brewery's 4,600 sq. ft. spacious warehouse setting, a 15-barrel brewhouse and brew system consistently creates new flavor recipes from the team, and Dr. Bill estimates the output around 280 barrels each month. The wooden barrel-aged program lies in wait, hibernating until the "beer tells you it's ready", and Preston's wooden barrel aging program allows wild yeast flavors

At Wild Barrel Brewing, there's plenty of room to find your own niche including the center oversize decorative barrel with tables and seats, as well as an outdoor patio.

The brewery team at Wild Barrel Brewing is devoted to fresh flavorful craft beers and sours. From right to left, Chris White, Preston Weesner, Bill Sysak, and Bill Sobieski.

to adjust for nearly two years. Each beer is poured at the tap in an unusual pear shaped snifter, allowing the beer to expand with its natural effervescence and aroma.

At the center of the tasting room interior and handcrafted by a local, Dave Nilsen, stands a gigantic wood-staved 20-foot diameter walk-in barrel serving as a circular photo gallery, plus adding intimate table seating. The brewery provides dining from local food trucks every Tuesday through Sunday. The brewery event facility may be booked for weddings and family gatherings, and it's freeway, family and dog friendly, and outdoor patio seating to enjoy. There is an adjacent sports complex business to wander around in, and visiting the brewery is a virtual breeze with freeway frontage and plenty of parking right off Hop Highway 78 in San Marcos, from the Woodside Valley Exit.

Open at 11am, the Wild Barrel Brewing tasting bar offers freshly made sessionable craft on tap, with outrageous flavors of 'Vice' fruit sours. There's an added varray of traditional West Coast IPAs, Imperial Stouts, and lighter Pilsners.

In Miramar, Duckfoot Brewing Co. invites customers to the brewery for an array of specialty gluten-reduced hop forward beers with a zesty, crisp taste.

The vault door to Societe's barrel-aged beer and sours opens to a carefully maintained temperature controlled climate.

CHAPTER 2

SAN DIEGO'S COLORFUL CRAFT

Concept, Color, Taste, Flavor

San Diego's craft displayed at Second Chance Brewery framed by the "Organization of a Craft Collective" in an exhibit made from found glass, metal, wood and paint by Bociek & Bociek Studios.

It's the Water

Among the four main ingredients used for brewing beer, the most plentiful possesses secrets your local craft brewer would like you to know. Conditioning or changing the molecular balance of water has been a customary way achieving perfection brewing beer. In other words, the water at the brewery is also handmade and changed through filtering or stripping it down to its very basics. Using a process called RO, or reverse osmosis, results are purified water striped of its inert active ingredients. Then, according to a beer's profile, PH, whether hard or soft in quality, the brewer may add back flavor "ions," elements or ionic salts to build water matching the formula of a traditional beer style. It's well recognized in San Diego there is a hard quality to the water in using it, and especially taste, and works well in its natural hardness for lusty dank IPAs. Its what's amazing about America's Capital of Craft, as well as a relaxing seaside destination.

Genius of Grains

Malted grains add basic body to a beer and depending on the type of malt used in brewing will impart in deep sweet roasted flavors. During the malting process grains are germinated then roasted. At the brewery, malted grains are carefully milled into a course grist in preparation to brewing beer. Yeast and enzymes are introduced during brewing process and consumes and converts the malt's proteins into alcohol and CO_2. When water is added to the recipe's ingredients and heated in the kettle, and malted grain becomes the perfect digestible food source for yeast pitched in during the process. The fermenting malt, water and yeast create a soupy wort ready for brewing into beer.

The Next Hop

Grown on trellises in full sun, hop vines produce flowering resinous cones used for strengthening and preserving a beer's flavor. It was used on board ships during the early centuries of tall ships discovering the New World at the beginning of international trade and commerce. There are varied percentages of resins, oils, tannins, pectins, nitrogen, dextrose and fructose available in hops. The most valuable constituents are resins contained in the plant's flower cones. Hops are a perennial plant producing vines reaching over 20-foot lengths from seeds bred from male and female plants. The latter produces compounds found in fragrant esters, flavors and aromas. Historically, hops were brewed in ales carried on board square-rigged tall ships supplementing the water supply. The ales transited the British Isles to India via packets, evolving into IPA styles we are familiar today. There are at least 170 varietals of hops, with many varietals used for brewing beer. Specific strains are added for a characteristic pungent bitterness.

At the turn of the century, California breweries had expanded along with a surge in population. An entry from the 1912 edition of the The Western Brewer and Journal of the Barley, Malt and Hop Trades states: "There are eighty-four California brewing establishments representing an investment of $30 million, paying employees annually $11 million. Materials used were Barley, 160 million pounds, Hops, 2.6 million pounds, and other materials amounting to 9.6 million pounds, yet in the face of these figures, there are people, unthinking and fanatical, who will vote for measure tending to the destruction of this great industry." Prohibition's conservatives clamped down within years and were responsible for closing all breweries nationally.

Why Yeast Matters

Yeast is a single cell member of the fungi family. Ubiquitous in nature, both wild and cultured yeasts are used in breweries worldwide. There are countless hundreds of strains and types, and it's the organism leads a curious life cycling through generations while exhibiting natural gathering tendencies into colonies, a tendency called flocculation. "Pitched" yeast goes into the cooling wort and begins splitting sugars in a process known as 'scarification' during the fermentation process. Many brewers have started classifying strains of yeast according to the aspects of individual taste, flavor, and characteristic aromas produced from varied strains. It's important characteristics will inspire brewers' recipes, thought out to a final ultimate beer generally ranked traditionally, or by styles, groups that have expanded into curious blends and curing possesses using metal kettles or wooden casks during the last years. Brewers require fresh yeast for brewing many gallons of beer. Therefore, there are laboratories in many breweries determining the quality, vitality, purity and health of developing colonies of yeast varietals. There are specialty businesses curating specific types of yeast, guaranteeing the quality and illuminating any impure processes wasting the beer, time and money.

Over a billion yeast cells fit on the head of pin, and the colonies feed on proteins, mineral salts, and starches, producing alcohol and carbon dioxide. CO^2 is a natural by-product outwardly visible in the thick foaming suds at the top of a beer. As sugars decrease during the fermentation process, used yeast begins settling and the beer will clarify. Because strains of yeast vary considerably in taste profiles, some also will begin feeding from the bottom up as lager yeast, and others fermenting from the top down are known as ale yeast. Relatives of ale and lager yeast are flavorful and sour fermenting microbe strains include lactobacillus, brettanomyces, diacetyl, and they're either entirely unwanted, or skillfully used for smoothing and souring beers. Yeast may be blended together or used as individual strains yielding varied brewing results.

New Beer

New beer flavors are often thought a renaissance in San Diego, as well as throughout the nation. The code of quality and purity historically regarded with an immovable adherence to its rules; called, 'Reinheitsgebot' (the German beer purity law) has been advanced. Brewers acquire the right equipment and attaining the correct ingredientsm, may brew any style of craft beer to perfection. The results are found at well attended competitions, such as the

Craft home brewers have congregated since 1992 at the Home Brew Mart, 5401 Linda Vista Rd., a crossroads for finding most brewing ingredients.

annual San Diego International Beer Festival, and The Great American Beer Festival (GABF), held at the Colorado Convention Center in Denver; and bring attention to the intense popularity favoring newer beer styles and classes.

During recent years, purveyors of West Coast San Diego fruit sours have formed fellowships of generational beer drinkers, and more increasingly evident, in 2020. Barrels are recycled from wineries, distilleries, or with even more specific labels like Four Roses whiskey or bourbon casks are used. Beer aging adds its 'new' processes of fermentation and blends with cultured or wild yeasts, and adjunct ingredients. Using varieties of herbs, fruits, yeasts, malts, hops, and each brew dry-hopped and steeped into crossover beers. There's avid attraction towards the latest wooden barrel-aged, kettle sours, lagers, stouts and hazy IPAs, celebrated by a relentless growth in the trade crafting fine beers to market. It's 'when the beer knows it's finished' applied as a rule commonly used by each barrel-aged brewer, produces 'out of the ordinary' results. Many new beers have succeeded and far exceed the possibilities used similarly in the wine industry's marketing of varietals, cellared and more exotic blends.

HOME BREWING IN SAN DIEGO

Quality Ale & Fermentation Fraternity

An Interview with Harold Gulbransen

There's no mistaking the members at San Diego's longstanding home brewing club, QUAFF, are among the most avid beer enthusiasts in the world. The story of Quaff is a remarkable accounting of long lasting bonds of friendship, and notably Harold Gulbransen's legendary stature during the course of the club's history. His encyclopedic information on world beer brewing styles and home brewing excellence makes him an integral member of San Diego's brewing legends. His recent trip to Belgium in late April 2017, continues the ongoing experience he's accumulated from visiting many European brewing capitals. This latest trip is no exception finding beer types that have influenced California's styles, as well as recent widening tastes toward American craft beers in Europe. Whether Abbey ales, saisons and dubbels, it's been the traditional recipes of yeast and blends of hoppy-malted flavors, and much closer to what we call craft beer in America.

Quaff formed in 1989, and regularly sponsors meetings, beer judging certification education, pub crawls, brewery tours, attending annual campouts at Anza Borrego Desert, and even Padre's tailgate parties each summer. At the beginning of the craft renaissance, the Home Brew Shop in El Cajon off Fletcher Parkway on San Diego's east side had opened a place where local home brewers went to buy supplies. A group of customers began meetings there and encouraged by the owner the group, considered forming a brew club helping to alleviate common problems and questions, unifying members into Quaff, San Diego's Quality Ale & Fermentation Fraternity.

As Harold recalled, "it was a way for the shop to disseminate the information and not having to spend the time one-on-one explaining the entire story of brewing and brewing systems. Craft beers require some knowledge and multiples of choices. The club accepts out of town members as it grows, "and because we are inclusive, our communications within embraces sharing with other members. Jamil Zainasheff, from Heretic Brewing Company, in the Bay Area up north has participated as a member for twenty years." Harold remembers his friend from the East Bay had discovered Quaff, "back when we got email addresses interconnected and exchange of ideas became more convenient. Now our membership hovers around 300 members and each enjoys the attitude of sharing secrets apparently some brew clubs might not."

Quaff's membership growth curve springs from conversations on-line, and when members chime in using direct knowledge, "normally solving problems about techniques or system recommendations, or maybe answering questions on water, recipes, or stylistic goals. So, the members' base of shared experiences end up helping and not making the same mistakes in another's home brewing." Harold expressed over 20 years he has been a Quaff member, there were memorable moments of home brewers bringing experiences of their own. "There are as many systems for brewing than there are home brewers, and each member may choose vastly different from the others. Ranging from the Porsche high-end computerized system - where you push buttons, or for guys like me with reconditioned '62 Chevy equipment cobbled together over lots of years, it's a hobby that even fits different personalities."

Harold pointed to some important distinctions on conditions with indigenous yeasts we associate with beers like hefeweizens and saisons. The hefeweizen yeast strain originated in Bavaria, a particular strain of wild yeast known for the banana-like tastes it adds. Unlike yeasts that are reclaimed, and then reused up to 10 different batches of beer, the hefeweizen strain does not behave like others because it mutates rapidly. "So, you never would use multiple strains from a single pitch of hefeweizen yeast unless from a reliable fresh source. Another factor with German brewing, beer was never brewed too late in the year because

Karl Strauss Brewery in La Jolla beer garden is open and a monthly meeting ground for QUAFF members, who share their recipes and comments in public forums on the process of brewing.

ambient bacteria would sour the beer. In Belgium. they brewed saisons in the spring when micro-flora were favorable and beers were made for the season. As crops of barley were harvested, they brewed and bottled beer for the upcoming winter. Often farmers added all kinds of things to saisons abundant at harvest time, like oats, wheat and spelt along with herb spices. Then, they'd bottle and bury it in the ground to keep it cool. It was used partly as pay to the migrant workers coming August through September and considered a part of the worker's nourishment. The brewer would deem a beer successful only if the spice present is indistinguishable without identifying a spice taste. The brewery wants you to know the beer is spiced and brewed accordingly to the season."

A classic brewery in Belgium known to Harold, Fantome in Soy, has brewed saison beers in four varieties for spring, summer, autumn, and winter; with saisons brewed typically lightly spiced, very pale, very effervescent and highly carbonated, and conditioned, a naturally carbonation for a flat beer in the bottle by adding small amounts sugar and yeast to each. Then, it is corked and sealed, so the yeast will ferment and create carbonation. "Quaff member, North Park Brewery's Kelsey McNair recently made an interesting take on a Belgian style Wit bier using local produce found at San Diego Farmer's markets making the way into the latest, greatest beers in town. He started with a Belgium styled Wit beer and used Buddha's Hand, a citrusy fragrant fruit from China, found locally. Traditionally, this style is ground coriander seed and grains of paradise, or white, pink, or black pepper in a wheat based beer. The style is a whole category in BJCP, and it's a spice, herbs and vegetable category. For instance, you can include pumpkin, or squash and root vegetables. I've made a sweet vicious potato beer, or a sweet potato Irish red ale with yams imparting a brilliant red amber."

Harold points out IPA was recently a subcategory of pale ale, "and now you have IPA as a category class including five different subcategories, English IPA, American IPA, Imperial IPA, Red IPA, and Pale Strong American Ale. In 2004, the first World Beer Cup was brought to San Diego, and I was asked by the Beer Association to be the Volunteer Coordinator, a job consisting of putting stewards and table captains together with the right beer at the right time, then in front of the right judges. It was a very complicated situation. Today's Quaff membership in San Diego promotes its study groups qualifying for exams with the Beer Judge Certification Program (BJCP.) It was not uncommon for brewers like local Grand Master Beer Judge, Peter Zien, entering and awarded coveted medals for their beers. As demand for craft beer in San Diego grew, each brewery had faced the challenge to increase production."

The GABF, or Great American Beer Festival has 90 beer styles in categories, and normally adjusts and modifies them each year. "Twenty years ago you would never think San Diego's brewers would ever have a successful influence on European beer, that would be impossible!" After Harold recalled a few late nights during the GABF of 2008, and another in 2012, where each followed up at pubs by conversations filled with visiting German and Belgium brewers' commentary. They compared the ultra-hopped IPAs they were drinking, and from what Harold heard, "a German's first reaction seemed disgruntled by the idea IPAs could be so out of balance; whereas, the Belgian's curiosity was piqued. By 2006, I saw the first Belgium IPA come up for sale and brewed as a more hop forward saison. It's become an official style as well. I can only attribute lessons learned in Quaff, and knowing how San Diego's influence of hop-forward style IPAs along and other advances. I've also seen certain breweries in Belgium brewing beers using only American hops, something you'd never imagine was possible 20 years ago!"

Harold has seen steady growth between 2008 to 2012, after breweries in San Diego County doubled, and the rise in local shelf space and tap rooms kept

The Home Brew Mart, 5401 Linda Vista Rd., San Diego

barrels rolling. "The guys at Stone had the right idea when they realized if it's good for the community of craft brewers, then it will eventually come around and be good for Stone to begin deliveries using refrigerated trucking nationally, not only for their own beer, but with virtually all the others from San Diego." One concern with the local brewers had been how to deliver its freshness from their high quality products to the market. And, for the home brewer, it's how to get the most out the brew. Even though it's purely agricultural, there are modifications you can always use with the available ingredients to make great beer. "It's a limitless palette with each ingredient and style you can decide to brew, unlike wine and dependency on that year's fruit harvest."

There are factors of creativity determining the output in San Diego's world of beer, and it is innovation and approach to a spectrum of styles. Another foundation to San Diego's beer industry is White Lab's International Headquarters, and member of Quaff for years. "Chris White was a PhD student at UCSD. I remember going to the Home Brew Shop, where you would buy a small amount of yeast and grow it to right amount; but, the store owner mentioned there was a new pitchable amount of yeast, ready to make a batch. It was Chris's invention starting a business in beer, and by the time he finished studying for the PhD, he didn't need to look for job." It's due to yeast strains dictating whether a beer is classified as ale or lager, as well as imparting a full range of hundreds of tastes. White Lab's tasting room and headquarters in Miramar is a brewery business inside San Diego poised with an international portfolio. Today's Quaff Home Brewing Club in San Diego may be regarded as the single most groundbreaking association of home brewers over the last decade. Historically, Harold has witnessed several member home brewers crossing over to professional brewing in San Diego from the club. The members keep alive the techniques of brewing through meeting and holding events, training, judging interacting under a single dedicated purpose of making unsurpassed quality beer styles through the lens of individual brewing perspectives. The unifying factor in San Diego's community of brewers signifies there's a clear passion and connectivity within the industry strongly supported in America's Finest City. "What's old is a lack of creativity. What we've witnessed from beer's past history, and you'd be bored just brewing Miller Genuine Draft all day long as a brewer. San Diego's totals over 130 breweries today has a scene defined by industry connections on social media connectivity, making a big difference. It's becoming increasing evident as Harold puts, "today, or anytime when I go into a brewery, I'm comforted I'll have great beer to drink."

The exhibit at Second Chance Brewery, "Organization of a Craft Collective" was made from found glass, metal, wood and paint.

Chapter 3
San Diego Brewing Affiliates

Golden Coast Mead

Oceanside Tasting Room
4089 Oceanside Blvd. Ste. H
Oceanside, CA 92054
760-630-4468

Julian Tasting Room / Julian Station
4470 Julian Rd.
Julian, CA 92036
619-433-5438
www.goldencoastmead.com

Frank Golbeck, Owner / Mead maker
Christopher Herr, Research and Development

Golden Coast Mead is the dream of mead maker, Frank Golbeck, after having grown up over decades visiting the family's San Bernardino apple farm. He recalls joyful moments being around his grandfather, a mead and fruit wine

vintner. Gatherings with the family included serving mead, an alcoholic beverage made from fermented honey, water and yeast. There are similarities to the traditions of brewing any classic craft beverage. It is perhaps one of the oldest brewed beverages known in history and when something old becomes something new again… Golden Coast's meadery was the first introduced on the Southern California scene. Opening in 2010, the meadery serves mead varieties with a characteristically light and refreshing taste of infused flavors made with a choice of fruits, spices,

and herbs. Each possibility adds distinct complexities, not unlike making a great honey wine varietal. Frank Golbek's story about his love of mead began after clearing the farm attic out with his Granddad. Among a few vintage wine bottles he found one serendipitous bottle of mead made by Grandad. It's the bottle Frank brought back to share with friends, and his fiancée. He recalls tasting, "sunlight in a bottle."

Mead's essence begins with a flower's nectar gathered by honey bees and adding a perfect yeast, water, herbs, spices and flavors, when intended. Golden Coast's crafted mead ranges between 6 and 14% abv and meant to be enjoyed while creating, adventuring or celebrating the joys of life. Golden Coast Mead uses top quality California honey, and Palomar Mountain spring water, making it a truly local product. Beginning in San Diego's Valley Center, Frank Golbeck crafts each mead into yielding spectacular tastes, making a delicious, gluten-free beverage. The process supports sustainable agricultural and honey bee populations. In 2010, mead making was hardly on the map save for a line or two picked out of a Tolkien novel. Craft beer became a visible force, yet meaderies were beginning to appear on the horizon. More than a whim, Golden Coast continues developing a showcase based on the goodness of mead making. The flavors represent the natural appeal of local honey. There are also specialties, one called Cyser, an apple cider - is a mead hybrid. A spiced mead, Golden Coast's Methleglin combines hibiscus with clove and honey. Tasting Room manager, Chris Herr explains, "We even may infuse spices and hops. We collaborated with Stone Brewing on Braggot, a hybrid mead ale using malt and dry-hopped flavors. We barrel-age the mead in French Oak, or with oak chips. Our Spiced Sour Mead, a 12% abv contains lactobacillus yeast, wildflower honey, ginger, cardamom and mace." It's a certainty, the family heritage preserved from Grandpa's 15-year old bottle once enjoyed by Frank, his wife and friends years ago, matches the nostalgic memories of family gatherings. Golden Coast's mead recipes continue to grow after 2014's opening of the Golden Coast Oceanside Tasting Room. Marine members at the Camp Pendleton Base find it a local, natural and preferred beverage. Mead fulfills expectations serving complex tastes and each perfected by the skills of the mead maker. A truly rewarding excursion into Middle Earth's laboratory takes you to Golden Coast Meadery.

BREWERY IGNITOR PROGRAM

H.G. FENTON COMPANY
A SAN DIEGO LEADER

H.G. Fenton Company
7577 Mission Valley Road
San Diego, California 92108
619-400-0120
www.hgfenton.com

Jacqueline Olivier, Commercial Property Manager
Bill Hooper, Commercial Portfolio Manager

Starting in 2015, H.G. Fenton's Brewery Igniter® Programs has opened the doors of seven craft breweries in San Diego. The well known real estate development and property management company, under the guidance of their team of skilled associates

has developed turn-key brewing systems with tap rooms to lease. The Igniter program fulfills a dream moving into a state of the art brewery outfitted with a unique tap & tasting room. The program has proven to sharply reduce start up costs, rapidly establishing a professional turnkey brewing facility.

H.G. Fenton's Commercial Portfolio Manager Bill Hooper explains, "The Brewery Igniter model helps reduce the upfront capital cost and risk associated with starting a new brewery by providing a turnkey brewing space and brewers just need to bring their recipes, business plan, marketing ideas and get licensed to sell their product. Without Brewery Igniter, brewers must finance expensive brewing equipment and bear significant construction costs, which means they

H.G. Fenton's North Park Brewery Igniter CRAFT building on El Cajon Blvd. operates with three individual breweries serving the freshest beer from custom Tap & Tasting Rooms.

carry significant debt for six months to a year before earning any revenue to pay it down. Since 2015, we have helped entrepreneurs follow their dream either starting up or expanding a brewery using an innovative solution that's flexible in allowing these people to enter or exit the market."

The Brewery Igniter program assists talented brewers building out individually designed facilities. The program provides up to 6,000 sq. ft. of space and includes fully installed professional brewing equipment. H.G. Fenton is one of a few companies equipped to handle and build a professional micro-brewery. Each brewery includes a comfortable tasting room and brewers can begin selling their beer sooner expediting the path to profitability. Anyone interested in fully outfitting a brewery and handling installations realize there are no guarantees avoiding the nightmares of plumbing or brewing equipment failures. The Igniter program finalizes all the steps and today, H.G. Fenton's brewery build-outs are running full-steam and open to the public in San Diego's neighborhoods of Miramar, North Park and Carlsbad.

San Diego's premiere Igniter location opened in January, 2016 at 9030 Kenamar Dr., in San Diego. One of two installations, Pure Project previously had been brewing craft beer in Costa Rica for over three years. Their Costa Rican

In North Park, the CRAFT Brewery Igniter with three breweries.

inspired brewing operation easily transitioned to the first Brewery Igniter in Miramar and up running in less than six months. A second San Diego craft brewery, Amplified Ale Works operates a popular brewpub in Pacific Beach. Each brewery was needing to expand crucial production facilities keeping up with demand for their beer. Brewery Igniter clients, Amplified Brewing and Pure Project reside in adjacent buildings, each with 7-barrel brew kettles, four 15-barrel brite tanks, four 15-barrel uni tanks, a two-stage glycolic chiller, malt mill, cold room, and three-station automatic keg washer. Both breweries have a tasting room and bar providing a treat to sampling unique San Diego craft beer.

CRAFT, by Brewery Igniter, became the second facility in San Diego located on 3052 El Cajon Blvd., celebrating a Grand Opening on November, 2016. The fully renovated vintage block building is located in the center of the North Park neighborhood, and the only craft brewing destination in San Diego designed for touring three different breweries under one roof! A family historical brewery, J & L Eppig Brewing Co. originally founded in 1866, operated in Brooklyn, NY. The brewery is reestablished as a family brewery, and reinvented.

Occupying the central CRAFT unit, Pariah Brewing Company features local brewmaster, Brian Mitchell's sophisticated talents and meticulously made beers. The third brewery on the corner is a local craft brewing pioneer, San Diego

Brewing Company, expanding production and visibility of their award-winning beer. Each brewery installation uses 10-barrel brewing systems created by Premier Stainless with two 20-barrel brite tanks, and five 20-barrel uni tanks, with a two-stage glycol chiller, malt mill, cold box and two-stage automatic keg washer. Each suite includes a complete boutique tasting room open to the public.

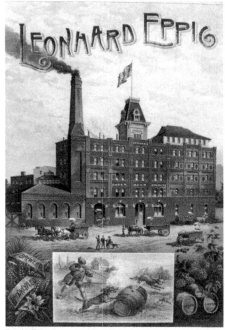

Brewery Igniter's latest location is in San Diego's North County coastal community of Carlsbad. Two breweries were opened in early 2017 at the 5840 El Camino Real and established in a quiet

Eppig Brewing was established in 1866 and revived in 2016, in San Diego using the Brewery Igniter programs.

warehouse plaza with plenty of parking. Rouleur Brewing Co. bends the rules of traditional brewing using European style yeasts with American beer styles and has gained the interest and support from the local Carlsbad cycling community. Wiseguy Brewing Company brings 10 years of home-brewing experiences into production, serving hoppy, German malty beer. Each brewery features a 10-barrel system with six 20-barrel uni tanks, two-stage glycol chiller, malt mill, cold box and two-stage automatic keg washer.

Rooted within the center of California's craft beer's capital, H.G. Fenton Company has been part of San Diego's community over a century. The company's solid understanding of the brewing industry issues supports entrepreneurial operations widely praised as a neighborhood economic engine. The company is consistently lauded for their development of the highest quality, modern equipped microbreweries. "We're proud to offer brewers an innovative solution supporting the industry's continued expansion and growth of San Diego businesses."

REAL BREWERS YEAST

The Future of Cultures
260 Via Del Norte
Oceanside, CA 92058
760-519-0849
www.realbrewersyeast.com

James Pfau, Ph.D.

Dr. James Pfau grows yeast cultures and genetically archives different strains of brewers' yeasts. It requires living cultures and nurturing microbial yeast with some sugar and chopped starches in a gelatinous kelp extract. The yeast colonies are generated inside a petri dish and the culturing process is called streaking. It's a term for inoculating a single yeast strain into a sterile environment. Then, James introduces them into flasks, where they grow into larger colonies, or "pitchable" quantities. The colonies are delivered in one liter containers to the breweries, and each strain is defined by different flavor characteristics making ales, lagers, kombucha, ciders, mead, wine and sake.

One billion yeast organisms may reside within a single dot in the dish. After brewer's yeast is added brewing wort, it digests proteins transforming the mixture by producing alcohol and carbon dioxide byproducts. To make more than a couple of milliliters of beer, one small dot in the fermentation kettle must be multiplied into gallons according to the beer recipe. And, if you're a client at Real Brewer's Yeast, you probably are looking for pure strains of yeast collected from traditional sources. Because contamination is possible, hundreds of yeasts are examined in the laboratory assuring purity and viability proven ready for the brewing process. Variant strains may cause entirely different tastes or off-flavors affecting the brew. Probabilities are increased by blending strains of yeast together and generating new and curious results. RBY swings to action supplying packaged quantities of yeast for fulfilling the recipes for San Diego breweries, and home brewers, or three to ten-barrel systems and larger. Each micro-colony responds to controlled temperatures and environmental conditions cloning authentic offspring from its "mother" colony cataloged and preserved in deep freeze storage.

After graduation from The University of Southern California's Ahmanson Center for Biological Research, James had focused his attention as a DNA scientist and a molecular geneticist. Then, one day, "an associate brought me her project with a bottle of Sierra Nevada Ale. In petri dishes, she had grown the California ale style yeast. It was a time I was messing around making synthetic DNA during the heyday of genetic engineering." The bottled beer brought the point home she had cloned yeast from the settled beer yeast transferred to the petri dishes! So, James immediately decided to take this strain into his own laboratory. It led to creating RBY 1 California Ale, a yeast originating from Pale Ale brewed back east. He went on to learn how to stock the yeast and growing cultures. American ales, Belgian ales and lagers are made from yeasts through genetically isolating, or a "backslap," the term capturing it from previously brewed batches in the past. Yeast remains alive and becomes dormant after brewing beer generally settling to the bottom. James explains, "Modello is my Mexican lager yeast is responsible for brewing Mexican lager. We supply the yeast for fermenting kombucha, wine, distillation, beer and certain types of yeast tolerating honey to make mead."

It's the vital role of yeast induced beverages that makes an important impact of the world of San Diego's brewing community. James works his wizardry with yeast on varieties for St. Archer Brewing, a major San Diego brewing company with a recently completed large expansion. "I began working with St. Archer at a time they were just a smaller tasting room. It takes 4000ml to brew a 10-barrel batch, and the yeast count averages 1.5 billion cells per milliliter. I've enjoyed the new hazy IPA craze, because it brings up the message of the important role of yeast critically affecting the flavors of a specific beverage. There is even beer brewed from Quinoa and using a malt that's naturally gluten free. You can even make beer from potato, rutabaga, strawberry or any other combination."

Dr. James Phau, a PhD scientist and owner of Real Brewers Yeast, supplies select strains of yeast for home brewing recipes and professional breweries.

White Labs compares examples of their craft beer using strains of yeast with surprising differences using similar recipes.

WHITE LABS GLOBAL HEADQUARTERS

9495 Candida Street
San Diego, CA 92126

Chris White, Ph.D.
CEO / Founder / President
858-693-3441
www.whitelabs.com

The modern science of White Labs Inc. delivers amazing ease, eloquence and evolutionary advancement concerning yeast, one of beer's four main ingredients. White Labs Headquarters in Miramar, established by owner Chris White, was started after years of home brewing experience and while working on graduate PhD studies at UCSD. A spark of innovation would change the future sourcing of yeast cultures and the art of brewing forever. Chris' idea was known as the first "pitchable yeast," simply growing pure strains anaerobically and delivering quantities made in pre-measured packages to brewers. Today, White Labs' bank of brewer's yeasts are used universally in pitchable quantities and available according to specific strains. A single package brews an entire batch or smaller home brewer amounts eliminate a brewer's need for a laboratory.

There are nearly 800 cultured strains of yeast to choose for an individual brewing profile, cultured and generated by White Labs with known characteristics of taste and aroma used in brewing craft beer. A single microbial yeast cell form colonies gathering together in a tendency called flocculation. They are classified as part of the fungus family, and their lifecycle depends on climatic conditions metabolizing the malted grain's proteins aided in the process by enzymes in brewing beer. As the yeast cells digest food, they naturally emit the byproducts of CO_2 or carbonation with alcohol, as the fermentation process turns brewed wort into beer. White Labs San Diego specializes in production of yeast strains and features a full analytical lab, offices and educational training rooms that are open to the public. The tasting room at White Labs provides an ultimate beer testing of tasting flavors from varied strains in the same recipes of beer. White Labs is the perfect place tasting freshly brewed American Pale Ale, Belgium, German, Australian ales and examining different yeast tastes. "This is why people come to the tasting room at White Labs, they order individual pints as one option, and we enjoy offering several different choices of beer using the same ingredient recipes changing up the brewer's yeast. It's a way to experience the difference flavors created by yeasts in a flight of four."

Some may think wood barrels are a thing of the past, but craft breweries have rolled out whiskey, wine and bourbon barrels in order to mature barrel-aged beer. Barrels at distilleries and wineries have added microorganisms creating unique flavors, also a specialty of White Labs. Each yeast example derived from a native source in nature represents either a known or wild harvested strain. There are customers coming to the laboratory with wild varieties they've collected to find or replicate the exact strain making a resulting beer. Then, White Labs cultures, stores and banks yeast producing pitchable quantities for the brewer.

White Labs' entry into professional brewing products in the San Diego area began in the mid-1990s, when trial packages were displayed at Ballast Point's Home Brew Mart in the Linda Vista area of San Diego. Back then, they carried just the WLP 001 California Ale Yeast® strain for 3 years, and it was always a sellout. Then, Chris White decided widening the types of yeasts he could make available, and today White Labs innovations developed the process for culturing yeast anaerobically making higher yeast cell counts remaining unexposed to external environmental conditions. The packs are available for the smallest to the largest of commercial enterprises. The yeast and fermentation company packages and ships pure brewers yeast via PurePitch®, a patented process of growing and shipping yeast in the same container. White Labs supplies 70 different strains of yeast for its customers each week. There is a 20-barrel brewery on-site that produces newly released and specialty beers featured in their 32-tap tasting room. Chris White's membership in San Diego's Quaff home brewing club from the mid-90s has played a pivotal role in support of the local craft beer and home brewing industry. A number of company programs support San Diego brewers and promote White Labs in the marketplace. The Customer Club rewards loyal home brewing customers, and another program greatly benefits hobbyists called the Freshness Certification Program. Friday at 6 p.m., the brewery is open in the tasting room for Trivia Nights, and a perfect educational stop offering facility tours daily.

At White Labs, quality control and mass production of yeast strains has grown from San Diego into an international enterprise.

Thanks for visiting

San Diego's Breweries...

&

Enjoy Beer More!

Chapter Four
Historical Spots and Neighborhoods

The downtown embarcadero makes travel and touring accessible within walkable areas to many attractions and museums.

Tour of San Diego

Driving south into San Diego County, passing Orange County's border on I-5, one of state's earliest founding sites on California's path of history may be seen at San Juan Capistrano Mission. First sight becomes visible of San Diego's gleaming Pacific ocean and the shores running nearly 70 miles south along San Diego's county coastline. You approach Oceanside and the exit for the harbor, Highway 76, and California's fourth longest wooden pier extending 1,942 feet into the Pacific. Not far are many suburban coastal communities with many breweries. When taking the alternative, I-15 South, driving from Temecula to San Diego county you drive past, Palomar Mountain rising a lofty 6,200 foot elevation at its peak, towering over North County. San Diego's hilly to mountainous terrain on I-15 meets State Highway 76 West, connecting to North County's Oceanside and the Pacific. The coastal backdrop extends south of many San Diego neighborhoods and industrial communities with roadways connecting a labyrinth of highways, leading to the industrial park locations of many craft brewery destinations. Also found are neighborhood clusters of tap & tasting rooms, within a 30-mile radius.

The first Spanish Europeans settled in San Diego in 1769 and created a system of inner-connected missions meant to lift the native cultures to a higher faith, and more pure ideals.

Touring the southern San Diego shores begins downtown at the founding site of 18th Century European explorers, and Franciscan Missionaries who arrived in 1769. They began settlements building colonies with unique mission buildings and pueblos reflecting the area's original culture. San Diego piers and its embarcadero are the city's most outstanding attractions and a 'Vacation Playland' of contemporary culture, museums, scenery, people, places, and destinations. Follow the blue and yellow Scenic Drive signs along 59-mile trail illustrated with a white sea gull, and take a fascinating route touring the town.

Early California

In recent times, the landmarks of California's earliest European heritage includes Spanish mission buildings, faithfully restored today. The first settlers adapted native traditional tule reed and thatched dwellings with mud-encased enclosures and rudimentary earthen floors. San Diego's aboriginal people, the Kumeyaay, Tipai and Ipai were people of white sage and eagle, living over past millennium within the diversified microclimatic regions of San Diego. Many native tribes were distinct cultures, woven together by over 100 unique languages. The first recorded exploration to Alta California was made by a Portuguese seafarer and contemporary of Hernando Cortés sailling from Mexico in 1542. Juan Rodriguez

A native uprising burned down the first 18th Century adobe mission, Mission San Diego de Acalá, after it was moved from the presidio site by Father Serra to its present location.

A popular San Diego city neighborhood, Little Italy, has many restaurants, shops, street festivals and brewery tasting rooms.

Cabrillo traveled along California's coastline under the Spanish flag and made notations off Catalina Island and San Diego's harbor, named Cape Mendocino to the north, and returned along the edge of the Big Sur coastline. Cabrillo landed in Los Angeles and Santa Barbara, claiming Spain's foothold in the New World. At sea, an accidental broken limb led to his fatal demise on San Miguel Island in the Santa Barbara Channel. Cabrillo never observed the Golden Gate or Monterey Bay during his explorations, and California ended up in near obscurity during the following centuries. Another little known explorer, Commander Sebastian Rodriguez Cerméno, brought three poorly constructed galleons in 1595, and wrecked the entire expedition on the rugged rocks during a failed attempt landing on the northern coast. Cerméno recovered 70 men and traveled by foot from Mendocino to Mexico, following the craggy treacherous California shoreline using makeshift vessels along the way. Leading a 1000-mile march, several new ports were discovered on the way.

Centuries later, the earliest Spanish settlements were founded by the legendary builder of the missions, Father Junípero Serra. He created colonies built by the native Indians, driven with the assumption to converting native culture into Christian civility. Father Serra founded Mission San Diego de Alcalá in 1769, and began a new land expedition to discover Monterey that included friars, an engineer, carpenters, Spanish leather-jacket dragoons, and Baja Indian interpreters leading a train of mules. The overland discovery party passed from San Diego to Santa Monica and Santa Barbara, San Luis Obispo and Paso Robles, extending a trail named by the friars, El Camino Real, or "The Royal Way," ending in Monterey, the capital city and presidio of Alta California. Blazed by missionaries in honor of the King of Spain, the path stemmed thousands of miles from the Guatemalan and Mexican jungles, connecting to Mexico City. The first violent unrest incited by mission neophytes stormed Mission San Diego de Alcalá and exacted the loss of several settlers including first friar, Franciscan Father Luis Jamye. Previous riots had been stopped by presidio soldiers defending the settlement, and many native lives were lost from measles and muskets. At one point, the rebellion erupted and ignited the mission buildings' rooftops with flaming arrows, devastating the entire San Diego mission. After Father Serra's return from Monterey, Mission San Diego de Alcalá was separated from the presidio and soldiers, and moved to today's location. In the present day, Mission San Diego de Alcalá was rebuilt at the site in 1803, then authentically restored during modern times using portions of the foundations and remaining

walls of the original. In 1888, an historical restoration of the 'Mother of the Missions' began in earnest, and an association formed aiming at the preservation of all missions, created in 1895. Work was carried through by the Land Marks Club, guided by Charles Fletcher Lummis, an influential newspaper writer who popularized California's earliest history. Sunday, September 13, 1931, marked the re-dedication of the 162-year-old mission church, as America tuned in to a live early national radio broadcast beaming a Pontifical High Mass from Mission San Diego de Alcalá during a two-day celebration. Downtown, on Friar's Road, a trip to Mission San Diego de Alcalá and the San Diego River makes a realistic journey into the frontier era of San Diego's founding.

Old Town State Historic Park

Near the west entrance of Mission Valley, Old Town State Park commemorates San Diego's earliest European settlement. Discover Old Town State Historic Park and visit the historic Spanish and Mexican historical buildings, serving as restaurants, museums and shopping facilities. Many Victorian buildings were scheduled for demolition but moved here and restored. Several parking lots are available and clearly marked, and many Old Town buildings are restored to their original beauty. You may stop at the Whaley House, Mormon Battalion, Casa de Estudillo, Seeley Stables, or Bazaar Del Mundo, to mention a few. There are free walking tours of Old Town State park daily. A popular landmark of locals and visitors alike, the park is filled with historical points of interest, quaint shops, and an abundance of Mexican and early California-style restaurants.

Seaport Village

Seaport Village along the Embarcadero has parking lots and street parking to visit the shopping center on the waterfront. Children enjoy rides on the restored 1890 Broadway Flying Horses Carousel, which like all carousels, rotates counter clockwise. The animals were carved by Charles Looft.

Old Town is a congregation of many restuarants, open markets, gift stores, museums and walkways through the original settlement in town.

Embarcadero

At the foot of Broadway is the Broadway Pier. From here, you may take walking excursions, rent bikes, and arrive at Seaport Village and ferry across to Coronado. The USS Midway Museum is docked at the wharf and open to the public for tours viewing the carriers aircraft collection. Further along the Embarcadero are vintage ships, submarines with tall ships at the San Diego Maritime Museum. The museum is afloat on a ferryboat, Berkeley, originally built in 1898. The ferry was a lifeboat for safely evacuating people, after the San Francisco earthquake of 1906. The tall ship, Star of India, was built in 1863 and is an iron-hulled square-rigger sailing vessel that has circled the globe 27 times. The latest re-creation built by the Museum is a galleon caravel ship, the San Salvador, constructed in honor of San Diego's founder, Juan Rodriguez Cabrillo. The San Diego Maritime Museum carefully modeled the ship after a 16th century ship that originally navigated California's coast. The boat was recently launched on its Maiden Voyage from Spanish Landing Harbor, and it departed retracing the past discoveries of the Golden State and Spain, in 1542.

Spanish Landing & Shelter Island

Adjacent to Harbor Dr., cross the bridge, stay in the right lane, go through the loop and continue driving west to Spanish Landing, a famous site of 1769. On your right is the "USS Recruit" or "USS Never Sail", were used to train recruits. Continue west and make a left turn on Scott St. This island is man made, and once a submerged shoal, today reflecting a nautical theme. Most of San Diego's sportfishing fleet is docked here. On the

The Star of India among the boats at the harbor during the 'Tall Ships' event on Labor Day weekend.

tip of the island you will find the Yokohama Fridendship Bell. Yokohama is San Diego's sister city in Japan. San Diego has several sister cities around the world. The Tuna Man's Memorial was dedicated in 1986, honoring the tuna fishermen who helped build San Diego's large tuna industry. The small beach has a walk along the marinas.

Harbor Island

One can find places for exploration driving north along the harbor to adjacent sites on San Diego's convoluted shoreline. Drive past the airport, Lindbergh Field, (named after Charles Lindbergh, whose famous flight began in San Diego) until you see the exit sign Harbor Island. Take the exit to see both ends of the island. Harbor Island is a man made island created by dredging the channel. There are several hotels and restaurants located there. The island is an ideal spot to walk or picnic downtown.

Along the embarcadero, the Star of India is docked at the San Diego Maritime Museum.

The Junípero Serra Museum of The San Diego History Center located in Presidio Park is a major symbol of the city atop the hill recognized as the site where California's first mission site and settlement was established.

Serra Museum San Diego

In 1769, overland expedition trails blazed from Baja converged on the founding site, San Diego's Presidio Hill. Pioneering the way, Capt. Don Fernando de Rivera marched 25 leatherjacket troops followed by 3 muleteers, and 42 Baja Christian Indians with Fray Juan Crespi, reaching San Diego's Presidio Hill and establishing California's first settlement. Father Junipero Serra arrived by sea, with a second party headed by military governor of Baja, Gasper de Portola and dedicated his first humble brush and mud mission, raising a cross at the San Diego presidio settlement. The Junipero Serra Museum displays early artifacts and photographs depicting San Diego. It is the presidio and first mission site with a panoramic view of Mission Valley, Mission Bay, and the San Diego metro area. Father Serra began Mission San Diego de Alcalá here, within the perimeter of a fort overlooking present day Old Town. Archaeological excavations have uncovered the site of the first church in Alta California, where Father Junipera Serra preached the gospel to the Kumeyaay Indians.

Hillcrest

After visiting the Serra Museum, continue up Presidio Dr. turning left at Arista St. Turn right at Fort Stockton. You are now driving through Mission Hills, one of San Diego's first suburbs. You will note the streets have names of birds. Turn right at Goldfinch. Continue one block, and turn left at Washington St., entering Hillcrest. At the turn of the century, Hillcrest was developed as the city up the hill from Old Town. In those days, many bankers lived there, and later was called "Bankers Hill". In this small community, there are many antique stores, art galleries, breweries, bakeries and restaurants.

Financial District

On Presidents Way, turn right onto Park Blvd. The street name will change to 12th Ave. Turn right at B ST., and enter through the Financial District of San Diego. Turn left on Fourth Ave., and right on Broadway. You are traveling west towards the waterfront.

Gaslamp Quarter District & Horton Plaza

During the California Gold Rush, this waterfront section was once known as the Stingaree District. It was here the saloons, gambling halls and opium dens opened their doors to sailors at nightfall. The area was also the home for most of San Diego's growing Chinese population. Visit the historical heart of San Diego called the Gaslamp Quarter. This 16-block area was the business district of Alonzo Horton's "New Town". In 1867, Horton, a native of San Francisco, bought 960 acres of mud flats and sagebrush for a total cost of $265.00, or 27¢ an acre. He developed it into what is now downtown San Diego. Because corner lots were more valuable, he made short street blocks. The area represents decades over the last centuries, and leads to Victorian and California style architecture. Note the fire resistant brick walls and metal shutters in the buildings. Many art galleries, restaurants, theaters and antique shops are located in this area. Street festivals are held throughout the year. Weekend guided walking tours of the Gaslamp Quarter start at the William Heath Davis house. This "salt box" house, as it was known, was built in 1859 in New England, shipped around Cape Horn and assembled here. It is the oldest standing prefabricated house in San Diego. Continue driving on Fifth Ave. and turn onto "F" St. At the next intersection, you are at Horton Plaza unique shopping, dining and entertainment complex. To visit this interesting site of contemporary architecture, park at the parking garage.

Point Loma

Standing 240 years over the originally named San Miguel Bay, the Cabrillo National Monument on both sides of the road has the gravestones of Fort Rosecrans Military Cemetery. Many of San Diego's men and women who lost their lives during wartime are buried here. A monument honors 60 sailors killed in the 1905 explosion of the gunboat USS Bennington here.

Sailing under the flag of Imperial Spain, Juan Rodriguez Cabrillo set out to search for the Strait of Anian, when California at the time was believed to be an island with passage linking the Atlantic and Pacific Oceans. On September 28, 1542, in command of two ships, the San Salvador and the La Victoria, he sailed into San Diego bay naming it

San Miguel after the Archangel Saint Michael. From the tip of Point Loma you can see Ballast Point, formerly known as Fort Guijarros (Fort Cobblestones), where trading ships loaded and unloaded cargo. Historians believe that Cabrillo anchored just inside Ballast Point. Sixty years later, on the feast day of the Franciscan Saint Didacus, or Saint de Alcalá de Henares, Sebastian Vizcaino renamed the port San Diego de Alcalá. There is a minimal fee to enter the park.

The old Point Loma Lighthouse began operating in 1855. Standing 462-feet above sea level, the light house was built with lights but, without a foghorn. It has been restored to its former residential style and is open to the public on special occasions. Because the original lighthouse was often obscured by fog therefore unable to guide ships into the bay, another lighthouse was built at sea level in 1891, and is still in use today. Naval research and a submarine base are located on Point Loma. The military, with its depression-proof payroll, was an economic savior during hard times. The tip of Point Loma is the most southwestern point of the continental U.S. During the winter months it is an excellent spot to watch Gray Whale migrations. Visit the tide pools, join in a ranger walk, see the auditorium, stop at the visitor center and enjoy the panoramic view of the San Diego harbor.

The San Diego Zoo

The world famous San Diego Zoo occupies 100 acres of Balboa Park. Dr. Harry Wegeforth founded the San Diego Zoo in 1916, with animals left over from the Panama-California Exposition. It is home today for more than 4,000 species of rare and endangered animals. Founders Day is celebrated the first Monday of October each year and admission to the Zoo is free. The exhibits feature animals in their natural shared environments. The zoo is best known for its conservation work. Research on the survival of endangered species is ongoing. For information about visiting the Wild Animal Park, also run by the San Diego Zoological Association in North County, is a popular attraction and national conservation effort to sustain many endangered species of wild animals.

Balboa Park

Balboa Park s
also known for
its gardens, picnic
areas, theaters and
sports facilities: golf,
tennis, horseshoes,
swimming and
shuffleboard. The
many museums in
the park are devoted
to art, history, space,
sports, physical

and natural sciences. A replica of "The Spirit of St. Louis", the plane in which
Charles E. Lindbergh crossed the Atlantic in 1927, is displayed in the Aerospace
Museum. Funding for the flight came from businessmen in St. Louis, Missouri,
hence its name. From El Prado, turn on Pan American Rd., East. The Spreckles
Organ Pavilion is on your left. Free concerts are performed here on Sunday
afternoons. The cluster of small cottages on your right is known as the Houses
of Pacific Relations. Each Sunday afternoon, one of the house's sponsors ethnic
folk dances, music or entertainment.

Balboa Park was designed adjacent to San Diego's metro area and designated as
a park in 1868. It's where the San Diego Natural History Center and Museum
was established in 1874. By 1892, landscaped by the early efforts of Kate Sessions
and her commercial landscape nursery near the park, her vision of many plants
and trees still remain there. By the turn of the century, the park was organized
with water systems and landscaping, and the name Balboa Park was adopted
in 1910, commemorating the name of the first European pioneer navigator to
Panama and first discoverer of the Pacific Ocean. The park hosted the 1915-
16 Panama-California Exposition, and many buildings were erected in the
Spanish renaissance style. The Museum of Man, Spreckles Organ Pavilion, and
1,500-foot long Cabrillo Bridge were early additions. During the California
Pacific International Exposition of 1935, and second World's Fair, featured art,
culture, architecture and gardens, establishing the park we are familiar with
today supporting museums, walkways and attractions in a beautiful setting
adjacent to the Fleet Center Space Center, and the renowned zoo. All roads
lead to surrounding neighborhoods, such as North and South Park, University

and Normal Heights. Other downtown
outskirts branch out from the metro
center, such as La Mesa just east via I-8,
past the first Spanish mission site and
presidio, museum and the town's first
settlement.

Ocean Beach

Return to Cabrillo Memorial Dr., and
the name changes to Catalina Blvd.
Continue driving and turn left at Hill
St. Continue and turn right on Cordova
St, which becomes Sunset Cliffs Blvd.,
and a popular surfing spot. At the base
of the cliffs are the tide pools and small
beaches. Taking a left turn onto Newport
Ave. extending all the way to the beach.

The concrete pier is the second longest in California, and an excellent spot for
fishing and bird watching. Still the quintessential 60's Beach Town…OB is
known to locals for its an original carefree feel. Surfers and surf shops abound
on Newport Ave., the town's main commercial street. Restaurants, breweries
and boutiques have opened and most of the businesses are locally owned.

Pacific Beach

On Mission Blvd., all cross streets are named after gems and minerals.
On your right is Pacific Beach, a popular and attractive beachfront for
sunbathing. If you wish to walk along the ocean front, stop at Diamond
Street. The beach is a great spot for people watching, skateboarding, biking
and roller skating. During WW II the ballroom on the 1000-foot-long
Crystal Pier hosted big band orchestras. Today you can stay at a motel and
fish from the pier. The Grunion, a native fish, spawns from March through
August and very popular with San Diegans. During the Grunion runs in
the evenings, hundreds of the female fish are carried by waves to the beach
where they lay their eggs in the sand. The male fish fertilize them seconds
later. The male and female fish are carried out by the next wave. During the
next high tide, about ten days later, the baby grunions hatch.

Mission Beach

The community of Mission Beach has the highest population density in San Diego. Continue driving along Mission Blvd. and at the Roller Coaster, turn right at the light and park. The Giant Dipper, 74 feet tall, is a historical landmark. You must be 50 inches tall to ride. Go for a swim in the indoor swimming pool, "The Plunge" in Belmont Park, or stop at one of the ocean front restaurants or shops.

Mission Bay Aquatic Park

Return to and continue driving along Sunset Cliffs Blvd., following the signs to SeaWorld Park. This area, originally known as Bahia Falso (False Bay), was developed in the 1950's. Today, this is a 4600 acre aquatic playground with 27 miles of beaches. To visit, continue driving across the bridge keeping to the right around the clover leaf, and drive North on Ingraham St. 135-acre marine life park features conservation efforts for dolphin, killer whale, otter and seal, with educational exhibits and aquariums. To continue the Scenic Drive, return to Ingraham Street and continue driving across two bridges. At the second bridge, which crosses over Fisherman's Channel, turn right onto Crown Point Dr. Stop and enjoy the wind surfers and catamarans flying across the water, or enjoy a walk on the pathway around the bay.

Soledad Mountain

Follow Crown Point Dr., turning left at Lamont St. At the intersection of Beryl St., the name will change to Soledad Rd. Drive up the hill past Kate Session Park, turning left onto Soledad Mountain Rd. Shortly thereafter, turn right onto La Jolla Scenic Dr. This is an exclusive residential area. Look for the turnoff to Mt. Soledad Park. At this lookout point, you can see San Diego County for miles in every direction. The Mt. Soledad Cross, 43 feet high , was dedicated in 1954 to honor the nation's war dead.

La Jolla Cove Park & La Jolla Cave

Continue in the same direction along La Jolla Shores Dr. and La Jolla Shores Beach, once known as "Long Beach". Turn right onto Torrey Pines Rd. A right turn at Prospect leads to the well-known shopping street in La Jolla. On Coast Blvd., drive to La Jolla Cove Park with its rock formation called Alligator Point. A lovely park for picnics, kite flying and other waterfront activities, the nearby Children's Pool, with its protective breakwater, is a safe seaside playground. Stop and visit the La Jolla Cave. Explore the cliff on top and view its vegetation and bird nests. The entrance to the cave is through the La Jolla Cave and Shell Shop. Walk down the stairs to visit the cave. La Jolla Underwater Park is an ecological preserve, that can only be reached by snorkelers from La Jolla Cove, and by scuba divers from La Jolla Shores.

Driving along Coast Blvd., turn right at Olivetas St., then the name changes to Pearl St. At the stop light, turn right onto La Jolla Blvd. At the stop light, turn left onto Nautilus, and drive up the hill and turn right onto La Jolla Scenic Dr. Turn left onto La Jolla Mesa Dr., and down the hill. Beautiful homes are on both sides of the road and the view of Pacific Beach and the coastline is magnificent.

UCSD Campus & Salk Institute

The UCSD Campus has technical schools featuring a different style of architecture. The magnificent library is located in an eucalyptus grove and is a spectacular sight. The faculty has many distinguished scholars and Nobel laureates.

Scripps Birch Aquarium

While in the UCSD area, you can take two short side trips from the marked Scenic route. First, the Birch Aquarium at Scripps, turn left from North Torrey Pines Rd. onto Expedition Way. Follow the signs. When you leave the Aquarium parking lot, turn left onto North Torrey Pines Rd. and take the second side trip, continuing north to the Salk Institute, named after Dr Jonas Salk. He had developed the polio vaccine. Just beyond the institute is the Torrey Pines Glider Port where the hang gliders sail through the air off the cliffs above the ocean.

The massive jawbone of a Gray Whale on display at the Scripps aquarium.

Coronado Island

Across the bay from downtown San Diego, fun and relaxation awaits in Coronado, San Diego's tropical island. Loew's Coronado Bay Resort offers acres of grounds miles from the hustle and bustle of daily life. A peaceful alternative to high rise hotels, the resort has three pools, hot tubs, and miles of beaches. Along with the myriad of activities we knew we'd find at Loew's resort, the pleasure of lolling away an hour or so gliding along the bay in an Italian Gondola is nearby. After enjoying a lovely dinner at the resort's dockside Market – settle down in the Gondola, with a plate of delectable chocolate dipped strawberries. The

The world famous Hotel Del Coronado.

Gondolier, dressed in full Italian regalia, rows out for a leisurely moonlight glide through the Coronado Cays. The water is often still, beautiful, as smooth as a sheet of glass.

The stately U.S. Grant Hotel on Broadway, in downtown San Diego.

SAN DIEGO NORTH COUNTY

Carlsbad Inn's breathtaking view of the sea.

Carlsbad

Carlsbad is a jewel in the necklace of Southern California's coastal communities. It is cultured, cozy, comfortable, and cordial. Enjoy a sunrise or sunset stroll along the promenade overlooking the water, or on the paved beach walk near the sand. With ample beach access, it is hard to pull away from water's edge, but the city has many other things to do, places to explore, and delights to be discovered. The famed La Costa Spa is here, as are many contemporary shops.

Do not miss the Museum of Making Music, which covers a century of music and its history. The museum displays many one of a kind instruments, and allows visitors to choose snippets from audio samples. They house over 500 classic instruments, including a piano that Al Jolson used to compose songs, and a Hohner accordion that Admiral Byrd took to the Antarctic in 1929.

Once just a flower farm, The Flower Fields became so popular with people who stopped to look at the Springtime rainbow of bright, colorful Tecolote Giant Ranunculus, they have instituted walking paths and a tractor ride through the fields -- antique tractors from the Vista Antique Gas and Steam Engine Museum pull open-air wagons. Fifty acres of flowers that have no fragrance, but it is a beautiful sight from near or far. The Flower Fields has roses and other blossoms, as well.

Some people think
LEGOLAND California
is just for kids. True, it is
a delight for youngsters –
dinosaurs, tame rides, and
waterworks – but watch the
faces of teenagers and parents,
and you see there is no age
limit for enjoying this special
place. It is hard to believe
that the Taj Mahal, a water-

blowing elephant, and more than 1,000 other models are "fa-brickated" from
30 million LEGO bricks. Miniland – a collection of cityscapes (built to scale)
– is intriguing. The U.S. Capitol building, a moving presidential motorcade, the
Golden Gate Bridge, Empire State Building, and a harbor scene cause eyes to
pop and mouths to hang open. The displays light up at night and have a number
of moving elements (such as a San Francisco cable car and New Orleans jazz
funeral). Everything except foliage is made from LEGO bricks – even tiny
ducks in a pond, people on benches, and a marching band.

For a relaxing mineral bath, facial, or massage, hasten to Carlsbad Mineral
Water Spa –Alt Karlsbad– on the site where therapeutic mineral waters were
discovered more than a century ago. After a number of years the mineral well
was capped. The current owners, Ludvik and Veronica Grigoras, reopened
the well in 1994 and created opulent surroundings – a Roman Caesar room,
Egyptian Cleopatra room, and Exotic Oriental room. Try a deep cleansing
Roman mud facial.

Oceanside

Oceanside is the headquarters preserving historic Route 101, and they are proud
of their buildings from the era when the highway was just beginning. The 101
Café, built in 1928 with a major remodel in 1954, continues to be a page from
history. Large photographs on the walls bring back memories of the era but the
old tabletop jukeboxes are now just for show. The Highway 101 preservation
society wants people to know and appreciate the history of where they live. He
reminds us that 101 was responsible for much of the development of California.
"We want you to recognize that when you are driving the route, it is more than
concrete …it has history." He calls it, "a Route 66 view, as far as you can sea."

North County's Safari Wild Animal Park is an important adjunct to downtown's San Diego Zoo renown for the preservation of endangered species.

Vista

A busy downtown with small shops, restaurants, condos, theatres and a progressive rebuilding of all streets and walkways. Vista's downtown and corporate areas near Business Park Drive has long harbored dozens of today's modern craft brewers. The old Paseo Santa Fe follows and crosses Hop Highway 78, in nearby San Marcos where many breweries are established.

Encinitas

Enter Encinitas and you're impressed by the re-creation of an old sign crossing 101, their main business street. This town has trendy shops and eateries, along with Swami's Point, directly below the gold domed minaret at the Hermitage gardens with an ocean view at the Self Realization Center.

Missions San Luis Rey & San Antonio de Pala

In Oceanside, along State Hwy 76, the Mission San Luis Rey de Francia was founded in 1798, becoming the 18th Spanish mission. Father Peyri was the architect and the mission covered nearly 8 acres of buildings. Productive harvests at the Mission San Luis Rey are well documented; an 1831 tally had noted its herds increased to 26,000 cattle, 25,000 sheep and over 2,000 horses, with 395,000 bushels of grain consumed. The settlement counted over 2,000

Mission San Luis Rey de Francia, Oceanside

barrels of mission wine. Due east, beneath the shadow of Mt. Palomar, Mission San Antonio de Pala's tall, 50-foot bell tower with its glorious melodic peel was heard as a beacon throughout the 19th century. Designated as a sub-mission to the San Luis Rey Mission, it had been established by Father Peyri with a granary in 1810, serving native Pala Indians as unto this day. A small chapel had been concescrated in 1815, and deemed a full mission maintained and decorated by faithful Indians. It was crafted from wood timbers and adobe brick, and continues today as a tradition of attendance started centuries ago.

Asistencia Santa Ysabel Church

Mission Santa Ysabel, lies along the trail to the northeast of Mission San Diego at a 3,000-foot elevation. After its long history of service, today it houses a more modern church. The first mass was celebrated on September, 1818 and led to building a mission chapel with several adobes, as well as establishing cemetery. Hung from a traditional scaffold, Mission Santa Ysabel church bells were perhaps the oldest of the entire mission chain, brought by early mission Indians on mules from San Diego. A museum is set up at the site today. Named Mission Santa Ysabel, honoring Elizabeth of Portugal of 1271, the location is just 35 miles from downtown San Diego, near the mining town of Julian. The mission featured a granary, several adobes, and served hundreds of Luiseño and Diegueño Indians from nearby foothills and mountains east of San Diego.

PUBLISHER'S STORYBOARD

There are many roads leading to great beer over past decades. Growing up in New Jersey, Robert A. Bellezza had the advantage of liberal laws passed in nearby New York City allowing an 18-year old drinking age. In the mid-1960s, doors opened to countless live jazz and blues spots, record shops in Times Square, and an occasional ticker tape parade ending with a 25¢ New York Pizza and 35¢ beer.

Stepping back to the city's timeless landmarks, one crusty old hangout and tap room established in 1854, McSorley's Old Ale House, represents one of many enjoyable trips, and New York's oldest continuously running brewery. It was exclusively open to men only until 1970.

The author, Robert Bellezza, age 9, with first camera.

The old barroom brewery offers either light or dark ale, served under its famous motto, "Be Good or Be Gone". From there, remain memories of frequent visits to Yankee Stadium and the amazing good fortune sitting at ground level at the first baseline of unforgettable days in the presence of Maris, Mantle, and Berra. Great baseball almost pleasantly was interrupted every 10 minutes by the hawkers' pitch over thousands of jubilant ball fans… "Beer Here! Beer Here!"

Moving to the Golden State from his native Garden State in 1967, Robert with his wife created a new home base in Sonoma County. As a book dealer and co-founder of California Tour & Travel in 1994, he began designing and distributing publications featuring well and lesser known California destinations and attractions. During 2013, "Papa Bob" settles into San Diego's North County's balmy climate near his favorite twin grandsons. Following the unmistakable swell of surf and suds rising within a torrent of over 140 incredible breweries producing artisan craft beer, it's practically an unavoidable pastime around San Diego. It's an unmistakable revolution touring and tasting rolled into one maverick wave of the finest quality craft flavors in San Diego, and the most amazing beers ever!

TASTING ROOM NOTES

BREWERY	NOTES
	32 North Brewing Co.
	Abnormal Beer Company
	Acoustic Ales Brewing Experiment
	AleSmith Brewing Company
	Amplified Ales Works
	Arcana Brewing Company
	Aztec Brewery Company
	Back Street Brewery
	Barrel Harbor Brew Company
	Bay Bridge Brewing
	Beach Grease Beer Co.
	Belching Beaver Brewery
	BNS Brewing & Distilling Co.
	Bolt Brewery
	Booze Bros. Brewing Co.

	Citizens Brewers
	Coronado Brewing Company
	Culver Beer Co.
	Dos Desparatos Brewery
	Duck Foot Brewing
	Ebullition Brew Works
	Golden Coast Mead
	Groundswell Brewing Company
	Indian Joe Brewing
	Iron Fist Brewing Co.
	Julian Beer Co.
	Kilowatt Brewing
	Latitude 33° Brewing
	Legacy Brewing Co.
	Little Miss Brewing
	Longship Brewery

	Mason Ale Works
	New English Brewing Company
	Nickel Beer Co.
	Novo Brazil Brewing Co.
	Ocean Beach Brewery
	Oceanside Brewing Company
	Pacific Islander Beer Co.
	Pariah Brewing Company
	Prohibition Brewing Company
	Pure Project
	Quantum Brewing Company
	Rip Current Brewing
	Rouleur Brewing Company
	San Diego Brewing Co.
	Second Chance Brewing Co.
	Smoking Cannon Brewery

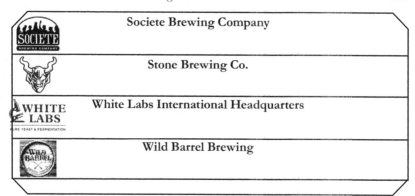

| Societe Brewing Company |
| Stone Brewing Co. |
| White Labs International Headquarters |
| Wild Barrel Brewing |

SAN DIEGO UNTAPPED!

BREWERY TAP & TASTING ROOM
EXCUSIONS IN AMERICA'S "CAPITAL OF CRAFT"

ALL INQUIRIES AND ORDERS:
ROBERT A. BELLEZZA

SDBEERBOOK@GMAIL.COM

Made in the USA
Las Vegas, NV
27 December 2022

64271759R00134